Also by Robert M. Sapolsky

A Primate's Memoir

The Trouble with Testosterone and Other Essays
on the Biology of the Human Predicament

Why Zebras Don't Get Ulcers:
A Guide to Stress, Stress-Related Diseases, and Coping

Stress, the Aging Brain,
and the Mechanisms of Neuron Death

MONKEYLUV

And Other Essays on Our Lives as Animals

Robert M. Sapolsky

SCRIBNER

New York   London   Toronto   Sydney

SCRIBNER
1230 Avenue of the Americas
New York, NY 10020

SCRIBNER and design are trademarks of Macmillan Library Reference USA, Inc.,
used under license by Simon & Schuster, the publisher of this work.

For information about special discounts for bulk purchases,
please contact Simon & Schuster Special Sales:
1-800-456-6798 or business@simonandschuster.com

DESIGNED BY ERICH HOBBING

Text set in Adobe Garamond

Manufactured in the United States of America

1   3   5   7   9   10   8   6   4   2

Library of Congress Cataloging-in-Publication Data

Sapolsky, Robert M.
Monkeyluv: and other essays on our lives as animals/Robert M. Sapolsky.
p. cm.
Includes bibliographical references.
1. Human biology—Popular works. 2. Genetic psychology—Popular works.
3. Sociobiology—Popular works. 4. Nature and nurture—Popular works. I. Title.

QP38.S275   2005
612—dc22   2005042534

ISBN-13: 978-0-7432-6015-2
ISBN-10: 0-7432-6015-5

"Nature or Nurture," "A Gene for Nothing," "The Genetic War Between Men and Women," "Why Are Dreams Dreamlike?," "Stress and Your Shrinking Brain," "How the Other Half Heals," "The Cultural Desert," and "Why We Want Their Bodies Back" were previously published in *Discover*. "Anatomy of a Bad Mood" was previously published in *Men's Health*. "Of Mice and (Hu)Men Genes," "Antlers of Clay," "The Pleasure (and Pain) of 'Maybe'," and "Revenge Served Warm" were previously published in *Natural History*. "Open Season" was previously published in *The New Yorker*. "Genetic Hyping," "Nursery Crimes," and "Monkeyluv" were previously published in *The Sciences*. "Bugs in the Brain" was previously published in *Scientific American*.

To
l.l., k.q.
f.s.

CONTENTS

CONTENTS

PART III:
Society and Who We Are

AUTHOR'S NOTE

The articles included in this volume appeared in various magazines, as noted in the table of contents. In some cases, articles appear here in slightly different form than originally published, and, in all cases, the text has been supplemented with "Notes and Further Reading."

ACKNOWLEDGMENTS

As noted, all of the pieces in this collection were originally published individually, in substantially similar form to what's presented here, in various magazines. A terrific consequence of this was that, in the process, I've gotten to work with some of the best editors in the business. And thus I thank Burkhard Bilger, Peter Brown, Alan Burdich, Jeff Csatari, Henry Finder, David Grogan, Marguerite Holloway, Emily Laber, Vittorio Maestro, Peter Moore, John Rennie, Rickie Rusting, Polly Schulman, and Gary Stix for their patience and skill in dealing with someone who should probably have been forced to take some English classes in college. Turning these individual articles into this book involved my getting to work with Colin Harrison and Sarah Knight at Scribner—it has been a pleasure to work with you, and I am grateful for your help in making it seem like these disparate pieces were actually meant to form a coherent whole. I thank my agent, Katinka Matson—this is our third book together, and she continues to be a great advocate and a wonderful judge of writing. Library assistance was provided by Kelly Parker and Lisa Pereira, and funds from the Bing Award and from the Hoagland Prize made it possible for me to initially ruminate over and eventually fulminate about these various topics.

PART I

Genes and Who We Are

Introduction

If your car breaks down, we all know the best way to fix it—you don't find someone skilled at doing an exorcism rite over the engine. Instead, you find someone knowledgeable who can take the engine apart, find the tiny piece that is the problem, fix or replace it, and put the whole thing back together.

If a violent crime occurs, with the perpetrator a mystery, we all know a good way to figure out what happened—you don't take a suspect, set fire to him at the stake, and if he burns to a crisp, conclude that that's a sign he was guilty. Instead, you take the mysterious event apart, find a witness who observed steps A through C, another who saw C through E, and so on, to piece together the whole picture of what happened.

And if your body breaks down, we know the drill as well—you don't sacrifice a cow to appease the spirit of the cousin who died while you owed her money. You get an expert who takes the illness apart and finds the tiny piece that is out of whack—the virus or bacteria, for example—and then fixes it.

The "solve a big problem by finding the itty-bitty thing that's buggered and fix it" approach is called reductionism—if you want to understand a complex system, break it into its component parts. Reductive thinking has dominated Western science for centuries, helped drag the West out of the quagmire of the Middle Ages.

Reductionism can be a great thing. Having been a kid early in the

Jonas Salk era, I'm mighty glad I got a fine product of reductive science, namely his vaccine (or maybe it was Albert Sabin's—let's not even go there), instead of having my pediatrician do a ceremony over me with some fetish gewgaw and goat innards to please the Polio Dybbuk. Reductive medical approaches have gotten us vaccines, drugs that block the precise step in the replication of a virus, have identified the precise piece of us that is broken in a variety of diseases. Our life expectancy has been extended to remarkable extents over the last century thanks to reductionism.

So if you want to understand the biology of who we are, of our normal and abnormal behaviors, the reductive approach gives you a pretty clear game plan. Understand the individuals who make up a society. Understand the organs that make up those individuals. Understand the cells that make up those organs. And way down at the foundations of the whole edifice, understand the genes that instruct those cells what to do. This approach gave rise to an orgy of reductive optimism in the form of the most expensive research project in the history of the life sciences, namely the sequencing of the human genome.

So genes seem to be pretty fundamental reductive building blocks of biology, including the biology of behavior. What does it mean to most people to say that a behavior "is genetic"?

That the behavior is innate, instinctual.

That the behavior is going to happen no matter what you do.

That (if you're operating in a public policy realm) you shouldn't bother wasting resources trying to prevent that behavior, because it's inevitable.

That (if you're a bit outdated about what evolution is about) the behavior is somehow adaptive, has some reason why it is actually a good and useful thing, reflects some sort of wisdom of nature, how an "is" is actually a "should be."

The first third of this book considers what genes have to do with behavior, with who we are. And you might already see where I'm heading, which is to debunk the ideas just listed, to show how little genes often have to do with the biology of who we are.

In the first essay, I consider what genes might have to do with one of the most important issues facing our troubled planet—explaining who gets into *People* magazine's special issue on the fifty most beautiful people in the world. As will be seen, there is a tragic paucity of good research in this area; I'll consider this book to have served its purpose if the first essay inspires even a single young scientist to tackle this daunting question.

The second essay, "A Gene for Nothing," introduces the reader to what genes actually do. As will be seen, you can't begin to understand the functions of genes without appreciating how the environment regulates those genes. Essay three, "Genetic Hyping," takes this theme in a different direction. One of the most important concepts in all of biology is that you can't really ever state what the effect is of a particular gene, or what the effect is of a particular environment. You can only consider how a particular gene and particular environment interact. "Gene/environment" interactions are so important that you can't be taught the biologist secret handshake until you use the phrase in conversation at least once a day. And like any concept that is that ubiquitous and foundational, it winds up getting ignored in all sorts of settings. Essay three tries to counter this, reviewing a study showing that imperceptibly subtle differences in environment can utterly change the effects of genes on behavior. Essay five, "Of Mice and (Hu)Men Genes," considers gene/environment interactions in fetal and early postnatal life and how they affect adult behavior, including in humans.

Amid all this gene-bashing, essay four, "The Genetic War between Men and Women," reviews a realm in which genes have some major effects on the development of brains, bodies, and behavior. In this case, the main point is that these genes are some of the weirdest ever uncovered, ones that violate all sorts of cherished beliefs in genetics. What is strangest is that they make perfect sense as soon as one recognizes that throughout evolution, there has been a genetic war going on between females and males, including human females and males. Warning: this essay does not make pleasant wedding-night reading.

Finally, essay six, "Antlers of Clay," returns to the foibles of relationships between the sexes. In species in which males and females go their separate ways after mating, all a female gets from a male are the genes contained in his sperm. The essay reviews how in many of these species males have evolved ways to advertise to females that they'd be great to mate with because of what terrific genes they have. And what females have evolved are ways to figure out if the guy is actually telling the truth. As we'll see, amid these intersexual battles over truth in advertising, genes may be getting a lot more credit than they deserve.

Nature or Nurture?
"The 50 Most Beautiful People in the World" Assess the Source of Their Good Looks

As a scientist doing scads of important research, I am busy, very busy. What with all those midnight experiments in the lab, all that eureka-ing, I hardly have any time to read the journals. Nonetheless, I stopped everything to thoroughly study the May 10, 1999, issue of *People* magazine, the special double issue, "The 50 Most Beautiful People in the World." It was fabulous. In addition to the full-color spreads and helpful grooming tips, the editors of *People* have gone after one of the central, pressing issues of our time. "Nature or nurture?" they ask on the opening page, as in, What gets you in our special issue? "About beauty, the arguments can be endless" (*P. Mag.* [1999] 51, 81). Best of all, the write-ups on each of the fifty contain some thoughts from the Chosen Ones or from members of their entourage (significant other, mom, hairdresser . . .) as to whether their celebrated states are a product of genes or environment.

Now, one should hardly be surprised at the range of answers that would come from a group that includes both a seventeen-year-old singer named Britney Spears and Tom Brokaw. What was striking, though, and, frankly, disappointing to this reporter was that our Fifty

Most Beautiful and their inner circles harbor some rather militant ideologues in the realm of the nature/nurture debate.

Consider first the extreme environmentalists, who reject the notion of anything being biologically fixed, with everything, instead, infinitely malleable with the right environmental intervention. There's Ben Affleck, newly arrived on the movie scene in the last few years, who discusses the impact of his pumping iron and getting his teeth capped. "Oh my God, you are a movie star!" one of his advisers is reported to have gushed in response to the dentistry (*P. Mag.* [1999] 51, 105). Mr. Affleck is clearly a disciple of John Watson, famous for the behaviorist/environmentalist credo, "Give me a child and let me control the total environment in which he is raised, and I will turn him into whatever I wish." It is unclear whether Mr. Watson's environmentalist hegemony included turning people into the Fifty Most with cosmetic dentistry, but a torch appears to have been passed to young Mr. Affleck. Thus, it hardly becomes surprising that Mr. Affleck's much celebrated affair with Gwyneth Paltrow, clearly of the genetic determinist school (see below), was so short-lived.

A strongly environmentalist viewpoint is also advanced by one Jenna Elfman, apparently a successful television star, who attributes her beauty to drinking one hundred ounces of water a day, following the teachings of a book that prescribes diets based on your blood type, and religiously making use of a moisturizer that costs $1,000 a pound. However, even a neophyte in the studies of human developmental biology and anatomy could quickly note that no amount of said moisturizer would result in the inclusion on *People*'s list of Walter Matthau or, say, me.

Then there is Jaclyn Smith, having moved into the stage of life where *People* mostly exclaims over the extent to which she still looks like the Charlie's Angel that she once was, explaining how her beauty has been preserved with good habits—not smoking, drinking, or doing drugs. This seems reasonable, until one reflects that that salutary nurturing of her self couldn't quite be the whole story, since no similarly ascetic Amish appears on the list of fifty. (A close friend of Ms. Smith's countered that her beauty is, in fact, maintained by her "humor, honesty, and unpretentiousness" [*P. Mag.* (1999) 51, 98], which left this reporter sincerely confused as to whether that should count as nature, nurture, or what.)

Perhaps the most extreme stance of this band is advanced by the actress Sandra Bullock, claiming that her beauty is all "smoke and mirrors" (*P. Mag.* [1999] 51, 81), a viewpoint that aligns her squarely with the Lysenkoism of the Soviet wheat experiments of the 1930s. One need merely to examine her work—for example, the scene in which she first takes the wheel of the bus in *Speed*—to detect the undercurrents of this radicalism in her oeuvre.

Naturally, similarly fringe opinions are coming from the opposing ideological faction, namely the genetic determinists among the Most Beautiful. Perhaps the brashest of this school is Josh Brolin, an actor whose statement would seem inflammatory to middle-of-the-roaders, but which could readily serve as a manifesto at the barricades for his cadre—"I was given my dad's good genes" (*P. Mag.* [1999] 51, 171). Similar sentiments come from the grandfather of the aforementioned Paltrow—"She was beautiful from the beginning" (*P. Mag.* [1999] 51, 169). Ah, young Brolin and Paltrow, an environmentalist adversary might counter, but what if your genetic destiny had encountered a good case of rickets or cowpox along the way, what magazine would you now be gracing?

The epitome of the natalist program, in which genetics is seen to form an imperative trajectory that is impervious to environmental manipulation, festers in the case of TV host Meredith Vieira. One is first told of various disasters that have befallen her—shoddy makeup application, an impetuous and unfortunate peroxide job on her hair—and yet, and yet, it doesn't matter; at each juncture, she is still beautiful because of her "phenomenal genes" (*P. Mag.* [1999] 51, 158). This reader, for one, blanched at the boldness of this analysis.

Finally, we consider Andrea Casiraghi, he of the Grimaldis of

Monaco, grandson of Grace Kelly. Amid the wonderment at his lovely complexion and classically sculpted cheekbones, the word comes out—"thoroughbred." Thorough*bred*. Oh, could it be so long before his advocates are pushing the eugenics programs that darkened our past? One searches the pages for a middle ground, for the interdisciplinary synthesist who would perceive the contributions of nature *and* nurture. Hope emerges with seventeen-year-old Jessica Biel, an actress celebrated for her skin, judiciously attributing it to her Choctaw blood *plus* getting regular facials with Oil of Olay.

And at last, one encounters one of the Chosen whose camp incorporates the most modern, most sophisticated and integrative insights concerning the nature/nurture conundrum, namely the idea that there is an *interaction* between genes and environment. For this, we consider a singer named Monica, who, despite lacking a last name, is not only one of the Most Beautiful People in the World, but apparently also one of the most important, because of the fame of an album of hers entitled *The Boy Is Mine* (a work unfamiliar to this reporter, whose association with popular culture ended somewhere around Janis Joplin). We are first informed about her wondrous skill at applying makeup and its role in gaining her acceptance into the Chambers of the Fifty. This, at first, seems like just more environmentalist agitprop. But then one asks, And where does she get this cosmetic aptitude from? Her mother supplies the answer: with Monica, "it's something that's inborn" (*P. Mag.* [1999] 51, 146).

One's breath is taken away at this incisive wisdom: *a genetic influence on how one interacts with the environment*. Too bad a few more people can't think this way when figuring out what genes have to do with, say, intelligence, or substance abuse, or violence.

⟶ NOTES AND FURTHER READING ⟵

At the end of each piece, I'll bring the reader up-to-date on any recent developments in the subject, reference the contents, and point to further readings.

This article, naturally, has become dreadfully obsolete, as is and should be the case with any such piece of investigative reporting by *People* magazine. Since that time, the fortunes of The Fifty Select have shifted. Ms. Elfman, I've dimly noted, seems to have appeared in a number of movies that tanked badly. Meanwhile, Mr. Affleck managed to spend at least two fifteen-minute blocks of fame as one-half of the world's most incandescently important couple, one so important that it even prompted the coining of a new word to describe it. Sadly, as a measure of his eclipse, current news (6/10/04) has been dominated by the revelation that J. Lo, at least this week, is married to someone else. And Ms. Spears, who only a few short years ago still had to be identified as "a singer," no longer needs an introduction for most readers; however, just around the time of career where most personal handlers would be convincing her that it's time for an image-burnishing trip to a Sudanese refugee camp as a special UN envoy, she is instead neurobiology's greatest teaching tool for demonstrating that the frontal cortex of the brain does not fully come online until around age thirty. As for what's happening with most of the rest of the Legion of the Select, I haven't a clue, not having had any idea who they were in the first place.

Lysenkoism—for those who haven't specialized in the "Embarrassing Chapter of Science" category of *Jeopardy!*—was a movement that dominated Soviet genetics for some decades. Named for the marginal geneticist Lysenko, it was an extreme environmentalist viewpoint in which organisms can inherit acquired traits (for example, be Caucasian and spend enough time in the tropics to get darkly tanned skin, and your offspring will be born with the same dark skin). This thinking was very much in line with Soviet environmental optimism, but didn't have the slightest shred of science supporting it, having been discredited before Darwin's time. This didn't prevent Lysenko from gaining vast influence over Stalin and agricultural planning. A bizarre episode in science that would just leave one shaking one's head in bemusement if Lysenkoism hadn't played a role in the death by starvation of vast numbers of Soviet citizens.

Further reading: the issue of *People* magazine cited above, of course, and as long as we're at it, the entire collection of *People* magazines. And for the best read on the science of this piece, see Matt Ridley's *Nature via Nurture: Genes, Experience, & What Makes Us Human* (New York: HarperCollins, 2003).

A Gene for Nothing

Remember Dolly the Sheep, the first mammal cloned from adult cells, in 1996? She was lovely, really an inspiration. She endured endless state dinners at the White House, all grace and cordiality. Then there was her triumphant ticker-tape parade down Broadway that won over even the most hardened New Yorker. Her appearances in those ubiquitous billboard ads for Guess? jeans (jeans, genes—get it? Those advertising guys are just awesome sometimes). Roller-blading at Disneyland for charity with the cast from *Friends*. Throughout the media circus, she was poised, patient, even-tempered, the epitome of what we look for in a celebrity and role model.

And despite that charm, people kept saying mean things about Dolly. Heads of state, religious leaders, editorialists, fell over themselves shortly after her debut to call her an aberration of nature, an insult to the sacred biological wonder of reproduction, something that should never remotely be considered in a human.

What was everyone so upset about? Some possibilities come to mind: (a) The Dolly Sheep/Dolly Parton connection unsettled everyone in a way that they just couldn't quite put their finger on. (b) Because the cloning technology that gave rise to Dolly could be extended to humans, we face the potential of droves of clones of someone running around, all with the exact same liver function. (c) Thanks to that technology, we might wind up with a bunch of clones who have the same brain.

Sure, the first two possibilities are creepy. But the dis-ease prompted by Dolly was overwhelmingly, remains overwhelmingly, about the third option. The same brain, the same neurons, the same genes directing those neurons, one multibodied consciousness among the clones, a mind meld, an army of photocopies of the same soul.

In actuality, people have known that this is not really the case ever since scientists discovered identical twins. Such individuals constitute genetic clones, just like Dolly and her mother (what was her name? Why does she get shortchanged in the media?), from whom that original cell was taken. Despite all those breathless stories about identical twins separated at birth who share all sorts of traits, like flushing the toilet before using it, twins do not have mind melds, do not behave identically. As one important example, if an identical twin is schizophrenic, the sibling, with the identical "schizophrenia gene(s)," has only about a 50 percent chance of having the disease. A similar finding comes from a fascinating experiment by Dan Weinberger of the National Institute of Mental Health. Give identical twins a puzzle to solve, and they might come up with answers that are more similar than one would expect from a pair of strangers. Hook those individuals up during the puzzle-solving to a brain-imaging instrument that visualizes metabolic demands in different regions of the brain, and the pattern of activation in the pair can differ dramatically, despite the same solution. Or get yourself some brains from identical twins. I don't mean pictures from a brain scanner. Get the real, squishy stuff, postmortem brains. Slice 'em, dice 'em, examine them with every kind of microscope, and every obsessive measure—the numbers of neurons in particular brain regions, the complexity of the branching cables coming out of those neurons, the numbers of connections among those neurons—and they all differ. Same genes, different brains.

The careful editorialists pointed this out about Dolly (and instead, some of the most disturbing issues about cloning raised by Dolly center on the possibilities of generating life simply for the purpose of banking away transplant-compatible tissues). Nonetheless, that business about identical genes supposedly producing identical brains tugs at a lot of people. And other gene/behavior stories keep getting propelled to the front pages of newspapers. One popped up shortly before Dolly with the report, headed by a Stanford team, of a single gene, called fru, that determines the sexual behavior of male fruit flies. Courtship, opening lines, foreplay, whom they come on to—the works. Mutate that gene and, get this, you can even change the sexual orientation of the fly. And that wasn't front-page news because of our insatiable fly voyeurism. "Could our sexual behaviors be determined by a single gene as well?" every article asked. And a bit earlier, there was the hubbub about the isolation of a gene related to anxiety, and before that, one for risk-taking behavior, and a while before that, the splash about another gene, whose mutation in one family was associated with their violent antisocial behavior, and then before that . . .

Why do these command attention? For many, genes and the DNA that comprises genes represent the holy grail of biology, the code of codes (two phrases often used in lay-public discussions of genetics). The worship at the altar of the gene rests on two assumptions. The first concerns the autonomy of genetic regulation. This is a notion that biological information begins with genes and flows outward and upward. DNA as the alpha, the initiator, the commander, the epicenter from which biology emanates. Nobody tells a gene what to do. It's always the other way around. The second assumption is that when genes give a command, biological systems listen. In that view, genes instruct your cells as to their structure and function. And when those cells are neurons, those functions include thought and feelings and behavior. And thus we are finally identifying the biological factors, so this thinking goes, that make us do what we do.

This view was put forward in a lead piece in the *The New Yorker* by a literature professor named Louis Menand. Mr. Menand ruminated on those anxiety genes, when "one little gene is firing off a signal to bite your fingernails" (the first assumption about the autonomy of genes, firing off whenever some notion pops into their head). He considers what this does to our explanatory systems. How do we reconcile societal, economic, psychological explanations of behavior with those ironclad genes? "The view that behavior is determined by an inherited genetic package"—the second assumption, genes as irresistible commanders—"is not easily reconciled with the view that behavior is determined by the kinds of movies a person watches." And what is the solution? "It is like having the Greek gods and the Inca gods occupying the same pantheon. Somebody's got to go."

In other words, if you buy into genes firing off and determining our behaviors, such modern scientific findings are simply incompatible with the environment having an influence. Sumpin's gotta go.

Now, I'm not quite sure what sort of genetics they teach in Mr. Menand's English department, but the sumpin's-gotta-go loggerhead is what most behavioral biologists have been trying to unteach for decades. Apparently with only limited success. Which is why it's worth another try.

Okay. You've got nature—neurons, brain chemicals, hormones, and, of course, at the bottom of the cereal box, genes. And then there's nurture, all those environmental breezes gusting about. And the biggest cliché in this field is how it is meaningless to talk about nature or nurture, only about their interaction. And somehow, that truism rarely sticks. Instead, somebody's got to go, and when a new gene is trotted out that when "firing off," "determines" a behavior, environmental influences are inevitably seen as something irrelevant that have to go. And soon, poor sweet Dolly became a menace to our autonomy as individuals, and there are perceived to be genes that control whom you go to bed with and whether you feel anxious about it.

Let's try to undo the notion of genes as neurobiological and behavioral destiny by examining those two assumptions. Let's begin with the second one, the notion that genes equal inevitability, generate commands that drive the function of cells, including those in our head. What exactly do genes do? A gene, a stretch of DNA, does not produce a behavior. Or an emotion, or even a fleeting thought. It produces a protein, where a specific DNA sequence that constitutes a gene codes for a specific type of protein. Now, some of these proteins certainly have lots to do with behavior and feelings and thoughts. Proteins include some hormones and neurotransmitters (chemical messengers between neurons), the receptors that receive hormonal and neurotransmitter messages, the enzymes that synthesize and degrade those messengers, many of the intracellular messengers triggered by those hormones, and so on. All vital for a brain to do its business. But the key is that it is extremely rare that things like hormones and neurotransmitters cause a behavior. Instead, they produce tendencies to respond to the environment in certain ways.

This is critical. Let's consider anxiety. When an organism is confronted with some sort of threat, it typically becomes vigilant, searches to gain information about the nature of the threat, struggles to find an effective coping response. And once a signal indicates safety—the lion has been evaded, the traffic cop buys the explanation and doesn't issue a ticket—the organism can relax. But this is not what occurs in an anxious individual. Instead, there is a frantic skittering among coping responses—abruptly shifting from one to another without checking whether anything has worked, an agitated attempt to cover all the bases and attempt a variety of responses simultaneously. Or there is an inability to detect when the safety signal occurs, and the restless vigilance keeps going. By definition, anxiety makes little sense outside the context of what the environment is doing to an individual. In that framework, the brain chemicals and, ultimately, the genes relevant to anxiety don't make you anxious. They make you more responsive to anxiety-provoking situations, make it harder to detect safety signals in the environment.

The same theme continues in other realms of our behaviors as well. The exciting (made-of-protein) receptor that seems to have something to do with novelty-seeking behavior doesn't actually make you seek novelty. It makes you more excitable in response to a novel environment than the folks without that receptor variant. And those (genetically influenced) neurochemical abnormalities of depression don't make you depressed. They make you more vulnerable to stressors in the environment, to deciding that you are helpless in circumstances where you are not (this particular point will be returned to in detail in essay five). Over and over it's the same theme.

One may retort that, in the long run, we are all exposed to anxiety-provoking circumstances, all exposed to the depressing world around us. If we are all exposed to those same environmental factors, yet it is only the people who are genetically prone toward, say, depression who get depressed, that is a pretty powerful vote for genes. In that scenario, the "genes don't cause things, they just make you more sensitive to the environment" becomes empty and semantic.

The problems there, however, are twofold. First, not everyone who has a genetic legacy of depression gets depressed (only about 50 percent—the same punch line as for individuals with a genetic legacy of schizophrenia), and not everyone who has a major depression has a genetic legacy for it. Genetic status is not all that predictive, in and of itself.

Second, only on a superficial level do we share the same environments. For example, the incidence of the genes related to depression is probably roughly equal throughout the world. However, geriatric depression is epidemic in our society and virtually nonexistent in traditional societies in the developing world. Why? Remarkably different environments in different societies, in which old age can mean being a powerful village elder or an infantilized has-been put out to a shuffleboard pasture. Or the environmental differences can be more subtle. Periods of psychological stress involving loss of control and predictability during childhood are recognized to predispose toward adult depression. Two children may have had similar childhood lessons in "there's bad things out there that I can't control"—both may have seen their parents divorce, lost a grandparent, tearfully buried a pet in the backyard, experienced a bully who got away with endlessly menacing them. Yet the temporal patterning of their two experiences is unlikely to be identical, and the child who experiences all those stressors over one year instead of over six years is far more likely to come with the cognitive distortion "There're bad things out there that I can't control, and in fact, I can't control anything" that sets you up for depression. The biological factors coded for by genes in the nervous system don't typically determine behavior. Instead, they influence the way you respond to the environment, and those environmental influences can be extremely subtle. Genetic vulnerabilities, tendencies, predispositions, biases. . . . but rarely genetic inevitabilities.

It's also important to realize the inaccuracy of the first assumption about behavioral genetics, the notion of genes as autonomous initiators of commands, as having minds of their own. To see the fallacy of this, it's time to look at two startling facts about the structure of genes, because they blow that assumption out of the water and bring environmentalism back into this arena big-time.

A chromosome is made of DNA, a vastly long string of it, a long sequence of letters coding for genetic information. People used to think that the first eleven letters of the DNA message would comprise Gene 1. A special letter sequence signaled the end of that gene, and then the next eleven and a half letters coded for Gene 2, and so on, through tens of thousands of genes. And in the pancreas, Gene 1 might specify the construction of insulin, and in your eyes, Gene 2 might specify protein pigments that give eyes their color, and Gene 3, active in neurons, might make you aggressive. Ah, caught you: might make you more *sensitive* to aggression-provoking stimuli in the environment. Different people would have different versions of Genes 1, 2, 3, and some versions worked better than others, were more evolutionarily adaptive. The final broad feature was that an army of biochemicals would do the scut work, transcribing the genes, reading the DNA sequences, and thus following the instructions as to how, eventually, to construct the appropriate proteins. Sure, we would torture our students with an entire year's worth of trivial details about that transcription process, but the basic picture suffices.

Except that that's not really how things work. The real picture, while different, does not initially seem earth-shattering. Instead of one gene coming immediately after another and all of that vast string of DNA devoted entirely to coding for different proteins, long stretches of DNA don't get transcribed. Sometimes those stretches even split up a gene into subsections. Nontranscribed, noncoding DNA. What's it for? Some of it doesn't seem to do anything. "Junk DNA," long, repetitious sequences of meaningless gibberish. But some of that noncoding DNA does something interesting indeed. It's the instruction manual for how and when to activate those genes. These stretches have a variety of names—regulatory elements, promoters, repressors, responsive elements. And different biochemical messengers bind to those regulatory elements and thereby alter the activity of the gene immediately "downstream"—immediately following in the string of DNA.

Aha, the death of the gene as the autonomous source of information, as having a mind of its own. Instead, other factors regulate when and how genes function. And what regulates this genetic activity? Often the environment.

A first example of how that might work. Suppose something stressful happens to some primate. There's a drought and not much to eat, forcing the animal to forage miles each day for food. As a result, it secretes stress hormones from its adrenals called glucocorticoids. Among other things, glucocorticoid molecules enter fat cells, bind to glucocorticoid receptors. These hormone/receptor complexes then find their way to the DNA and bind to a particular regulatory stretch of DNA, one of those operating instructions. As a result, a gene downstream is activated, which produces a protein that, indirectly, inhibits that fat cell from storing fat. A logical thing to do— while that primate is starving and walking the grasslands in search of a meal, this is the time to divert energy to working muscles, not to fat cells.

This constitutes a cleverly adaptive mechanism by which the environment triggers a genetic response that modifies metabolism. This is a very different scenario for thinking about where information originates in these cascades. In effect, these regulatory elements introduce the possibility of environmentally modulated if/then clauses: *if* the environment is tough and you're working hard to find food, *then* make use of your genes to divert energy to exercising muscle. And if a human refugee wanders miles from home with insufficient food because of civil strife, then the same is probably occurring—the behavior of one human, the sort of environment that that individual generates, can change the pattern of gene activity in another person.

Let's get a fancier example of how these regulatory elements of DNA are controlled by environmental factors. Suppose that Gene 4037 (a gene that has a real name, but I'll spare you the jargon), when left to its own devices, is transcriptionally active, generating the protein that it codes for. However, a regulatory element comes just before 4037 in the DNA string, and typically a particular messenger binds to the regulatory element, shutting down Gene 4037. Fine. How about the following: That inhibitory messenger is sensitive to temperature. In fact, if the cell gets hot, that messenger goes to pieces, unwinds, and comes floating off the regulatory element. What happens? Freed from the inhibitory regulation, Gene 4037 suddenly becomes active. Maybe it's a gene that works in the kidney and codes for a protein relevant to water retention. Boring—another metabolic story, this one having to do with how a warm environment triggers a metabolic adaptation that staves off dehydration. But suppose, instead, Gene 4037 codes for an array of proteins that have something to do with sexual behavior. What have you just invented? Seasonal mating. Winter is waning, each day gets a little warmer, and in relevant cells in the brain, pituitary, or gonads, genes like 4037 are gradually becoming active.

Finally, some threshold is passed, and wham, everyone starts rutting and ovulating, snorting and pawing at the ground, and generally carrying on. If it is the right time of year, then use those genes to increase the likelihood of mating. (Actually, in most seasonal maters, the environmental signal for mating is the amount of daily light exposure—the days are getting longer—rather than temperature—the days are getting warmer. But the principle is the same.)

A final, elegant version of this principle. Every cell in your body has a distinctive protein signature that marks it as belonging to you, a biochemical fingerprint. These "major histocompatability" proteins are important—this is how your immune system tells the difference between you and some invading bacteria and is why an organ transplanted into you that has a very different signature gets rejected. Now, some of those signature proteins can detach from cells, can get into your sweat glands, wind up in your sweat, and help to make for a distinctive odor signature. And for a rodent, now that's important stuff. You can design receptors in olfactory cells in a rodent's nose that can distinguish between odor proteins that are similar to its own versus ones that are totally novel. That's easy to construct—the greater the similarity, the tighter the protein fits into the receptor, like a key in a lock (to hark back to one of our great high-school science clichés). What have you just invented? A means to explain something that rodents do effortlessly—distinguish between the smells of relatives and strangers.

Keep tinkering with this science project. Now, couple those olfactory receptors to a cascade of messengers inside the cell that gets you to the DNA, to the point of binding to those regulatory elements. What might you want to construct? How about: if an olfactory receptor binds an odorant indicating a relative, then trigger a cascade that ultimately inhibits the activity of genes related to reproduction. You've just invented a mechanism to explain how animals tend not to mate with close relatives. Or you can construct a different cascade: if an olfactory receptor binds an odorant indicating a relative, then inhibit genes that are normally active that regulate the synthesis of testosterone. And what you've just come up with is a means by which rodents get bristly and aggressive when a strange male stinks up their burrow, but not when it's the scent of their kid brother. Or you can design the olfactory receptors to distinguish between odor signatures of same-sex individuals versus those of the opposite sex, and before you know it, this is a mechanism to regulate reproductive physiology. If you smell someone of the opposite sex, then start that cascade that ultimately gears up those genes down in the gonads—and there's reasonably good evidence that that mechanism works in humans as well as in rodents.

In each of these examples, you can begin to see the logic, a beautiful sort of elegance that couldn't be improved on much by teams of engineers. And now for the two facts about this regulation of genes that dramatically change how to view genes. First, when it comes to cells in mammals, by the best estimates available, more than 95 percent of DNA is noncoding. *Ninety-five percent.* Sure, a lot of that is the junk packing-material DNA, but your average gene comes with a huge instruction manual about how to operate it, and the operator is often environmental. With that sort of percentage, if you think about genes and behavior, you have to think about how the environment regulates genes and behavior.

And here's the second fact. A big deal when it comes to genes and evolution and behavior is the genetic variation between individuals. By this, I mean that the DNA sequence coding for any given gene often varies from one person to the next, and this often translates into proteins that differ in how well they do their job. This is the grist for natural selection: Which is the most adaptive version of some (genetically influenced) trait? Given that evolutionary change occurs at the level of DNA, "survival of the fittest" really means "reproduction of individuals whose DNA sequences make for the most adaptive collection of proteins." And the startling second fact is that when you examine variability in DNA sequences among individuals, the noncoding regions of DNA are considerably more variable than are the regions that code for genes. Okay, a lot of that noncoding variability is attributable to the junk packing-material DNA that is free to drift genetically over time, because it doesn't do much. After all, two violins must look fairly similar, whether one is a Stradivarius and the other a Guarneri, whereas packing material can be as different as old newspaper or Styrofoam peanuts or bubble wrap. But there seems to be enormous amounts of variability in regulatory regions of DNA as well.

What does this mean? Hopefully, we've now gotten past "genes determine behavior" to, more typically, "genes modulate how one responds to the environment." What that business about 95 percent of DNA being noncoding implies is that it is at least as valid to think something like "genes can be convenient tools used by environmental factors to influence behavior." And what that second fact about variability in noncoding regions means is that "evolution is mostly about natural selection for different assemblages of genes" is not as accurate as thinking that "evolution is mostly about natural selection for different genetic sensitivities and responses to environmental influences."

By now, ideally, it should seem mighty difficult to separate genetic and environmental factors into neat, separate piles. Just as it should be. Sure, some cases of behaviors are overwhelmingly under genetic control. Just consider all those mutant flies hopping into the sack with some cartoon cricket. And some mammalian behaviors can be pretty heavily under genetic regulation as well. As a remarkable example, there are closely related species of voles that differ as to whether they are monogamous or polygamous, and it all has to do with the receptor for a particular sex-related hormone in one part of the brain—monogamous male voles have that receptor there, polygamous voles don't. In an amazing piece of tinkering, some scientists expressed that receptor in the brains of the polygamous males—who were now monogamous (with it not being clear whether making males monogamous should count as gene "therapy").

These cases of single genes truly having a major influence on a behavior are usually cases where the behavior is carried out in pretty much the same way by everyone. This is a necessity. If you plan to pass on copies of your genes, there can't be much tolerance for variability in these behaviors. For example, just as all violins have to be constructed in fairly similar ways if they are going to do their job, all male primates have to go about the genetically based behavior of pelvic thrusting in fairly similar ways if they plan to reproduce successfully. (Yup, I just compared violins with pelvic thrusts. Yet more evidence for why those science majors should be forced to take an English class now and then.) But by the time you get to courtship or emotions or creativity or mental illness or you name it, it's an intertwining of biological and environmental components that utterly defeats the notion that somebody's got to go, and it's not going to be genes.

Maybe the best way to finish is to give another, particularly striking example of how individuals with identical genes can, nonetheless, come up with very different behaviors. I'm a bit hesitant to reveal this, as the finding has only recently surfaced, and it hasn't been published yet. But, what the hell, it's such an interesting finding, I have to mention it. Remember the massive public opinion poll that was carried out in 1996, the one that canvassed the opinions of every sheep throughout the British Isles? The researchers recently broke the code and identified the questionnaires from Dolly and her mother. And get a load of this bombshell: Dolly's mother voted Tory, listed the Queen Mum as her all-time favorite royal, worried most about mad cow disease ("Is this good or bad for sheep?"), enjoyed Gilbert and Sullivan, and endorsed the statement "Behavior? It's all nature." And as for Dolly? Voted Green Party, thought Prince William was the cutest, worried most about "the environment," listened to the Spice Girls, and endorsed the statement "Behavior? Nature. Or nurture. Whatever." You see, there's more to behavior than just genes.

—◌ NOTES AND FURTHER READING ◌—

Dolly, sadly, died in 2003 at age seven, very young for a sheep. She seemed to suffer from some sort of syndrome of premature aging— "a sheep in lamb's clothes" in one striking, poignant description. This precocity occurred for reasons that are still not fully understood but may have to do with her DNA being prematurely worn. The ends of the DNA that constitute chromosomes are called telomeres. With each round of cell division, telomeres get a bit shorter, and when they get below a certain threshold of length, cell division ceases. It could well be that Dolly started off life with the telomeric "clock" in each of her cells already at her mother's age. Suffering from a variety of ailments, she was put to sleep, and her early demise stands as a cautionary note for cloning enthusiasts.

Numerous basic textbooks go over the broad features of how genes are organized and how they function. For one of the classic texts, see Darnell J, Lodish H, and Baltimore D, *Molecular Cell Biology* (New York: Scientific American Books, 1990).

For information about how the heritability of schizophrenia and of major depression are both about 50 percent, see Barondes S, *Mood Genes: Hunting for Origins of Mania and Depression* (New York: Oxford University Press, 1999).

The subject of fruit flies and genes about sexual orientation is reviewed in Baker B, Taylor B, and Hall J, "Are complex behaviors specified by dedicated regulatory genes? Reasoning from Drosophila," *Cell* 105 (2001): 13. The study where polygamous voles were made monogamous is Lim M, Wang Z, Olazabel D, Ren X, Terwilliger E, and Young I, "Enhanced partner preference in a promiscuous species by manipulating the expression of a single gene," *Nature* 429 (2004): 754.

For an overview of the genetics of behavior (including anxiety and risk-taking behavior), see Plomin R, *Behavioral Genetics,* 3rd ed. (New York: W. H. Freeman, 1997).

For two superb overviews of how the function of genes cannot be understood outside the context of environment, see Moore D, *The Dependent Gene: The Fallacy of "Nature versus Nurture"* (New York: Owl Books, 1999) and Ridley M, *Nature via Nurture* (New York: HarperCollins, 2003).

Genetic Hyping

Spring is in the air, the new fashion season is upon us, and once again genes are all the rage. A great example is a recent report by a group of scientists at Princeton, led by Joe Tsien, which was published in *Nature,* one of the two most prestigious and influential general science journals in the world. The scientists did some molecular biology magic with some mice—engineering them so that neurons in one part of their brains had an extra copy of a particular gene. The neurons there made abnormally large amounts of the protein coded for by that gene, a protein that is part of a receptor for a neurotransmitter that appears to play a key role in learning and memory. And remarkably, the animals scored significantly higher than ordinary laboratory mice on an array of memory tests. The mice, it seemed, were genetically engineered to be abnormally smart.

This was great science: important subject, slick techniques, careful documentation. And some good marketing whimsy by the scientists as well, who called the mouse Doogie, after television series wunderkind D. Howser of some years back, who was so precocious that he had graduated med school by age fourteen.

The whole thing made a big splash with the media. Desk editors, who had exhausted every possible pun about Dolly the cloned sheep, had to find clever ways to work Doogie into the headline. Pundits erupted with the obligatory essays about whether parents should want their children to be Doogie mice in time for preschool entrance exams. And *Time* magazine, which at least showed some restraint in placing a question mark after the "The IQ Gene" headline, made it a cover story.

That's great. But I'm not here to go on about the Doogie mouse. Instead, I want to focus on another paper about genes and behavior that was published around the same time in the equally prestigious journal *Science.* That paper, in contrast, attracted little notice from the media, and what attention it did get seemed wrongly directed. In fact, the commentaries managed to completely miss the point.

Genes, of course, have plenty to do with behavior. Genes determine your intelligence and your personality, and certain genetic profiles cause criminality, alcoholism, and a proclivity toward misplacing car keys. Hopefully, three essays into this book, you know this is a total crock, medieval genetic determinism. Genes don't cause behaviors. Sometimes, they influence them.

With that out of the way, we can flout our sophistication. Genes influence behavior, environment influences behavior, and genes and environment interact—a point that I'm hammering at over and over. What that means is that the effects of a gene on an organism will usually vary with changes in the environment, and the effects of environment will vary with changes in the genetic makeup of the organism.

I say *usually* because a powerful influence from one side of the interaction can overwhelm the other. In the realm of intellect, for example, even the most salutary environment will not compensate for the catastrophic consequences of, say, the genetic makeup that leads to Tay-Sachs disease. And conversely, some environmental influence can overwhelm the effects of genetics. Even the most impressive genetic pedigree of smarts isn't going to do you much good if you're subjected to severe and prolonged protein malnutrition during childhood. But in the less extreme realm, genes and environment happily interact, achieving a balance.

*   *   *

The cleanest way to study gene/environment interactions is to hold one-half of the interaction constant, modify the other half systematically, and then see what happens. Manipulating the environment can be relatively straightforward—all of us have known about that ever since our mothers objected to the friends we were hanging out with back when. But the controlled and selective manipulation of genes is hot stuff, the world of Web site headlines and twentysomething molecular-biology geeks becoming gazillionaires when their biotech companies go public. Newfound techniques of the genetic trade—inserting into an animal a gene from a different species, to create a so-called transgenic animal; replacing one of an animal's own genes with a nonfunctional version, to make a "knock-out" animal; even selectively mutating one of an animal's genes—are flashy and exciting.

In recent years, molecular biologists have manipulated the genes in mice that code for neurotransmitters (the chemicals that carry messages between brain cells), as well as the genes for neurotransmitter receptors (molecules that reside on the surface of a cell and react to incoming neurotransmitters). Altering those genes, biologists have found, can affect such aspects of mouse behavior as sexuality, aggressiveness, risk-taking, substance abuse, and more. Is it such a jump to infer that the same link between genes and behavior could exist for people?

But often, on closer examination, it turns out that the evidence supporting the asserted links between genes and behavior is slight. For example, as mentioned in the previous essay, starting around 1996, a series of studies was published linking a particular gene in humans to novelty-seeking behavior, and the media went wild over this. However, these studies showed, collectively, that this gene accounted for only about 5 percent of the variability in the data.

Now, people tend to crave—and consequently overvalue—virtually anything new. The result is a pretty widespread impression among the lay public, who (through no fault of their own) learn their science in ten-second sound bites, that it takes dramatic and extreme environments to blunt the influence of genes.

This is where that study published in *Science* comes in. No *Time* cover story, no catchy mouse nicknames. The study was a collaboration among three behavioral geneticists: John Crabbe, of the Veterans Affairs Medical Center and Oregon Health Sciences University, both in Portland; Douglas Wahlsten, at the University of Alberta in Edmonton; and Bruce Dudek, at the State University of New York in Albany. Crabbe and colleagues had a modest goal: they wanted to standardize the various tests that have been devised to measure the effects of genes on such mouse behaviors as alcohol craving and anxiety. The investigators' aim was to identify tests that would measure the effects accurately enough to give results that were highly reproducible from one lab to the next.

To do so, the team created uniform conditions in their three labs. First, each investigator used groups of mice from the same eight strains (a strain is a pedigree of mice in which close relatives are mated with each other for umpteen generations, until eventually the animals are about as alike as identical twins). Some were control strains; others had undergone some kind of fancy genetic manipulation, such as having a gene knocked out. The key point is that these strains had already been studied. It was common knowledge, for instance, that Strain X was your basic, off-the-rack strain used in many labs, Strain Y was more prone than other mice to drinking alcohol when it was offered, Strain Z tended to be anxious, and so forth.

Once the experimenters were sure they had acquired identical strains of mice, they took steps to make sure the mice were raised in standardized conditions. No unnoticed advantage or disadvantage— a more delicious brand of food, say, or a particularly dirty cage—was to be allowed that might cause the mice to act differently from one another for reasons that had nothing to do with genes. Finally, the experimenters chose six standardized behavioral tests—tests that trapped the mice in mazes, forced them to swim to safety, or imposed some other task whose success or failure is readily measurable.

That was the game plan. But the execution was an obsessive's heaven. Crabbe, Wahlsten, and Dudek did cartwheels to make sure that these animals were tested in identical environments in all three labs. They standardized every element of the process—from the way the animals were raised to the way the tests were conducted to the equipment that was deployed. For example, because some of the mice were born in the lab but others came from commercial breeders, the homegrowns were taken for a bouncy van ride to simulate the jostling that commercially bred mice undergo during shipping, just in case that sort of stressor had an effect.

The team tested animals of exactly the same age (to the day) on the same date at the same local time. Animals had been weaned at the same age, all their mothers had been weighed at the same time. They all lived in the same type of cage, with the same brand and thickness of sawdust bedding, which was changed on the same day of the week. When handled, it was at the same time and by human hands in the same type of surgical glove. They were fed the same food, kept in the same lighting environment, at the same temperature. And when their tails were marked for identification, it was always with a Sharpie pen. The environments of these animals could hardly have been more similar if Crabbe, Wahlsten, and Dudek had been identical triplets separated at birth.

What the three geneticists created was a world of genetically indistinguishable mice raised in virtually identical environments. If genes were all-powerful and deterministic, one might expect that there would be complete replicability of scores within and between labs. All the animals of Strain X would have gotten six points on test one, twelve points on test two, eight points on test three, and so on, regardless of which lab they were tested in. The mice from Strain Y would also perform in a uniform manner, getting, say, nine points on test one, fifteen points on test two, and so on. Such a result would constitute convincing proof that genes are massively deterministic of behavior . . . at least for the genes in question . . . in these mice . . . on those particular tests.

But that's absurd—no one would have expected anything as extreme as the precise same results on a test from each animal. Instead, the expectation would have been something close: perhaps all the animals of Strain X would get roughly similar scores on test number one in all three labs—a statistical dead heat. And that's precisely what occurred for some of the strains, when they were administered some of the tests. In one test (the most impressive example), nearly 80 percent of the variability in the data across all three labs could be explained by genetics alone. But the truly critical finding was that for some of the tests, the results gave no support to the assertion that genes make mice what they are, let alone make us who we are. In fact, the results on those tests were sheer chaos—the same strain differed radically from lab to lab (though the results within labs were mostly uniform).

Just to give you an example of the sorts of numbers these guys got in some of these cases, take a strain with the uncuddly name of 129/SvEvTac, and a test in which the effects of cocaine on a mouse's level of activity is measured. In Portland, cocaine caused these mice to increase their activity an average of 667 centimeters of movement per fifteen minutes. In Albany, an increase of 701. Pretty good— similar result. And in Edmonton? More than 5,000 centimeters of activity, by genetically identical mice in a meticulously similar environment. That's like a set of triplets competing in a pole-vaulting competition. They've all had the same amount of training, all have the same night's rest, the same breakfast, all are wearing the same brand of underwear. The first two manage 18-feet and 18-feet-1-inch pole vaults, and then the third one launches himself 108 feet into the air.

Now, there might be some ways to explain these discrepancies. One might breathe a sigh of relief, for instance, if all the data were utterly random—if the results for any given test within a given strain within a given lab were so variable from mouse to mouse that no pattern could be detected. Then you could be reasonably sure that the tests must be lousy and poorly defined, or there weren't enough animals tested to begin to discern patterns, or maybe Crabbe and buddies don't actually know squat about the arcana of mouse behavioral testing. But some of the data, as I noted, were quite similar within tests, within strains, and within labs. These guys knew what they were doing with their mice.

Another possibility is that some of the results differed from site to site because of the nature of the places themselves. Maybe the mice in Albany differed from the mice at the other two labs because they were dispirited by the architecture of the hideous state capitol (on account of early environmental influences as a native of New York City, I'm obliged to consider Albany a dive). Maybe proximity to those amber Canadian waves of grain in Edmonton would do something systematic to those mice. But no, that couldn't be it either, because the discrepancies in the data across all tests were not systematically attributable to any of the labs.

And a third possible explanation: perhaps the difference in behavior within strains of mice was merely a matter of degree. Suppose some mouse strain is known to exhibit an atypically large amount of Behavior X. Maybe the problem was that at sites one and two, those mice showed vastly more of Behavior X than did the control mice, where at site three, they showed only a little bit more than the controls did. But no, the data were far more chaotic than that: for certain tests, the strain in question showed more of Behavior X than the controls did at one test site, the same amount as the controls at the next site, and less than the controls at the third.

Or, a fourth possibility: perhaps the environmental conditions were not, as some of the critics suggested, as perfectly synchronized as they seemed to be. A group of scientists wrote to *Science* to suggest that the size and texture of the mouse-chow pellets might have been at fault. Another group argued that the key uncontrolled variable was that the graduate student who oversaw the testing in Edmonton was allergic to mice and so wore a space-suit-like protective helmet—they went on to advance a rather exuberant hypothesis about the possible interactions between behavioral genetics and the ultrasound emitted by the motor on the helmet's air filter. And, yes, it turns out that there was, indeed, a crucial slipup in all the careful controls: the colors of the Sharpies used for marking the animals were inconsistent—some were black, others were red. Could that have been the extreme environmental influence that skewed the results?

Excuse my facetiousness, but I am troubled by the fact that all too frequently, investigators are reluctant to reject their dearly held preconceptions and allow their expectations to impose blinders. When the Crabbe team's paper was published, it was accompanied by a commentary written by one of the journal's staff writers, under the title of "Fickle Mice Highlight Test Problems." In it, the writer bemoans how hard it will be to deal with the problem of tests that don't give the expected result.

This seems all turned around to me. If the behavioral tests fail to show a reliable genetic effect, the first conclusion that jumps to mind shouldn't be that the tests need some fixing. If environmental variables that are too subtle to be detected in a study as thorough as this can markedly disrupt a genetic effect on a behavior, then there's not much of a genetic influence going on here. Or maybe none at all.

The moral is that one should not get too excited about some new genetic component of behavior until the effect has been replicated in a number of different places and with a broad array of tests—something that is seldom done. Instead, what happens is this: A team of scientists do some fancy molecular tinkering in a batch of mice. They manipulate a gene relevant to the brain, and, well, after all that impressive work, something must be different about the animals. Test them, and lo and behold, some behavior does turn out to vary in a statistically significant way on one test. Aha, an effect, a splashy publication, and when the next lab can't replicate it, the onus of proof can easily shift to identifying their "test problem." That scenario has been played out for many of the wonder genes. The conclusion must be that many published accounts linking groups of genes to specific behaviors could well be off base.

Don't get me wrong and overestimate how much I'm trying to bash genes. Genetics influences neurobiology, behavior, every facet of biology, and to extraordinary extents in some cases. The data in this study demonstrate it pretty convincingly for some of the strains and behaviors. There's just the danger of expectations running away with you, even among the supposedly hard-nosed science community. It is most certainly not the case that this new genetic emperor has no clothes.

But amid our current near-feverish interest in genes, especially among the lay public, it's worth noting that the emperor is a bit less accessorized than usually assumed. The environment, even a subtle one, can still more than hold its own in the biological interactions that shape who we are.

⟿ NOTES AND FURTHER READING ⟾

The development of the Doogie mouse was reported in Tang Y, Shimizu E, Dube G, Rampon C, Kerchner G, Zhuo M, Liu G, and Tsien J, "Genetic enhancement of learning and memory in mice," *Nature* 410 (1999): 63. The paper by Crabbe and colleagues was "Genetics of mouse behavior: interactions with laboratory environment," *Science* 284 (1999): 1670. The "Fickle Mice Highlight Test Problems" commentary, by Enserink M, can be found in the same issue, page 1,599. The Crabbe paper documents some of the remarkably detailed efforts they made at standardizing conditions in the three different labs. Further information was provided in a Web site that they set up (www.albany.edu/psy/obssr). The letters published in response to the Crabbe paper can be found in *Science* (1999): 285, 2,067–70.

The demonstration that the gene related to novelty-seeking behavior accounts for only about 5 percent of the variability in the data in humans can be found in Ebstein R and Belmaker R, "Saga of an adventure gene: novelty seeking, substance abuse and the dopamine D4 receptor 9D4DR) exon III repeat polymorphism," *Molecular Psychiatry* 2 (1997): 361.

Demoralizing postscript: A few years after the Crabbe et al. paper was published, I found myself sitting in the office of a Nobel laureate, whose work should have made him cognizant of this science. This was one huge alpha male of a baboon, and I was terrified of him, wildly intimidated. No doubt the stress of the situation was gravely impairing the executive functioning of my frontal cortex (stay tuned for what that's about) and my ability to make a prudent decision, because I decided to bring up the Crabbe paper. "So what did you think of that Crabbe paper in *Science*?" I ventured enthusiastically. A blank look. "You know, the paper where they were testing the different mouse strains at the three different labs . . . ?" I offered. A cold, blank look. I was dumbfounded—he seemed not to have heard of the study, which hadn't, after all, been published in some biology newsletter in Estonian. I launched into a description of the methods and results of the study. He made a snarfly sort of exhaling sound through his nostrils and said something to the effect of, "It sounds like they don't know the first thing about how to do basic behavioral testing." Thank God, my time was soon up with him and I was allowed to scuttle out of his office before my imprudent frontal cortex had allowed me to say what I thought of his attitude about an inconvenient scientific finding.

The Genetic War
Between Men and Women

As most newlyweds quickly learn, intimate relationships, even the most blissful, can buzz with tension. Couples typically find themselves struggling over money, in-laws, ex-lovers, and how much the woman's placenta should grow when she is eventually pregnant. That last one is a killer. The guy wants his woman to have a fast-growing placenta, while the woman thinks this is just some guy ego thing and does all she can to keep it down to a reasonable size.

Amazingly, a conflict along these lines seems to get played out in various mammals, including us. And it turns out that this is only the tip of the iceberg of a bizarre world of battling between the sexes, where males and females have conflicting evolutionary goals. Understanding that the struggle takes place can explain a lot of strange behavior and physiology, and give us insights into some diseases and maybe even about our nature as a species.

A male and female, even a mating pair, have a remarkable potential for disagreement, for having non-overlapping goals. This point was first appreciated by the general public when Jimmy Cagney smashed the grapefruit in Mae Clarke's face in 1931. Scientists, who rarely go to movies, took a few more decades to begin to grasp this. For them, it required the routing, in the 1960s, of a style of evolutionary thinking termed group selection. This is the Marlin Perkins peaceable kingdom where animals behave "for the good of the species." This usually turns out to be crock—closer examination shows that behavior is more readily explained by a combination of two phenomena. First, "individual selection," where organisms try to maximize the number of copies of their genes that they pass on to succeeding generations (prompting the quip "Sometimes a chicken is just an egg's way of making another egg"). Second, "kin selection," where one helps closely related individuals to pass on copies of their own genes (prompting the quip "I'll gladly lay down my life for two brothers or eight cousins").

The conflict is rooted in two facts. First, that a mating pair of animals are not related (most species do some pretty elaborate contortions to make sure that close relatives don't mate with each other) and thus don't have a whole lot of evolutionary incentive to cooperate with each other. Second, that a very asymmetric bill is related to reproduction—females have to pay the metabolic costs of a pregnancy, plus a ton of maternal behavior in some species, while males merely have to fork up the calories to pay for sperm and whatever their species' equivalent is of a couple of pelvic thrusts. Bad mate choice on his part, and he's out a coupla sperm; bad choice on her part, and she's spending forever wiping the noses of these funny-looking kids with the questionable genetic makeup.

Now imagine a mating pair in a species where, once they mate, the male clears out, never to be seen again. Over time, males mate with numerous females, females with numerous males. This opens up a particular arena of conflict. What would be the logical thing the male has been selected for? To evolve traits that maximize the survival of any offspring of this mating, at all costs, even at the cost of the mother's future reproduction. After all, he's never seeing her again, what does her future stake in the Darwinian stock market concern him? Zilch. In fact, if what makes these kids of his more likely to survive *decreases* her future fertility, even better, since she is likely to be mating with some other, competing male. That's his logic.* And what's hers? A more complex one, in which she would, of course, like the offspring of this mating to survive and thrive, but where that must be balanced with her future reproductive success. For example, among mammals, nursing inhibits ovulation. So a mammal mom wouldn't want to nurse this kid for the rest of her life, even if doing so greatly increased its chances of survival. Otherwise, she might never again ovulate, become pregnant, and bear more young.

This conflict is played out viciously among fruit flies. Rather than growing old in each other's arms, drosophila mate with multiple partners, none of whom stick around for a second date. And look at what they've come up with: male's semen contains toxins that kill the sperm of other males. Mate with a female who has recently mated with someone else, and the spermicide goes to work, killing competitors' sperm. Great adaptation. But the trouble is that the stuff is toxic to the female and gradually harms her health. This doesn't bother the male at all. It increases his evolutionary fitness, and he's never going to see her again. Caveat emptor, baby.

William Rice, a biologist at the University of California at Santa Cruz, did a wonderfully slick experiment in which he kept female Drosophila from evolving, while letting the males compete against each other. After forty generations, he had selected for the most evolutionarily "fit" males, who had the most offspring and the strongest

---

*As an important and obligatory caveat that should seem familiar to readers interested in this sort of biology, the individual animal does not sit there with an evolution textbook and a calculator. This is not an arena of *conscious* strategizing by the animal. Instead, phrases like "The animal *wants* to do this, *decides* that this is the time to," and so on are a shorthand for the more correct but cumbersome "Over the course of evolution, animals of this species who, at least in part through genetically influenced mechanisms, are better able to optimize the timing of this abandonment behavior leave more copies of their genes, thus making this attribute more prevalent in the population." The personifying is just an expository device agreed upon to keep eveyone from falling asleep during conferences.

toxic punch in their semen. Critically, females who mated with them had a shorter life expectancy.

And what is the female strategy with all this? That became apparent as Rice did the converse study—now, hold the males constant and let the females evolve against Mr. Toxic Crotch, and what do you know, in roughly the same number of generations, the females had evolved away the shortened life expectancy, developing mechanisms to detoxify what the male had come up with. Touché. There's an unforgiving, coevolutionary arms race going on here.

What is new and challenging is the bizarre landscape in which the same is occurring in mammals, including us. And these involve genes called imprinted genes, which seem to violate the basic tenets of genetics.

Back to high-school biology—Gregor Mendel and dominant and recessive genes. Mendel taught us that genetic traits are coded for by "Mendelian" pairs of genes, one from each parent. He figured out how the pairs of genes interact to influence the organism, depending on whether the pair has identical or differing messages. And in the classical Mendelian world of genetics, it doesn't matter which parent contributed which genetic message. Get the vanilla version of a gene from a mother and the chocolate version from the father, or the other way around, and the trait that the pair of genes codes for in the offspring will look the same.

Imprinted genes violate Mendel's rules. With these genes, only the gene from one parent has input—the matching gene from the other parent is silenced, losing its influence over the trait expressed. Most experts in this new field believe that there are only a couple hundred of these genes in humans (out of our total of roughly thirty thousand), but they can be quite influential.

Very odd stuff. A wonderful, clarifying light helps pull together much of this weirdness, as there is an intriguing pattern to what most of the characterized imprinted genes do. Those all have something to do with growth—of the placenta, the fetus, or the newborn. And the genes derived from the father favor greater, faster, more expensive growth, while the maternally derived genes counter their exuberance. In 1989, the evolutionist David Haig of Harvard first suggested that imprinted genes—including these genes in humans—are a case of intersexual competition, fruit-fly sperm wars redux.

The first battleground is the placenta, a tissue that can seem more than a little creepy. It's only partially related to the female, but it invades (a term used in obstetrics) her body, sending tentacles toward her blood vessels to divert nutrients for the benefit of this growing creature. The placenta is also the scene of a pitched battle, with paternally derived genes pushing it to invade more aggressively while maternally derived genes try to hold it back. How do we know this? In rare diseases, maternal or paternal genes related to placental growth are mutated and knocked out of action. Lose the paternal input, and the antigrowth maternal component is left unopposed— you get diseases where the placenta never invades the mother's endometrium, so the fetus has no chance to grow. In contrast, remove the maternal input and let those paternal genes run wild unopposed, and you get placental invasiveness over the top—a stupendously aggressive cancer called choriocarcinoma. Thus, normal placental implantation represents an uneasy stalemate.

The imprinting struggle continues during fetal development. One gene that codes for a powerful growth-stimulating hormone in rodents is expressed only by a paternally derived gene. This is a classic case of Dad pushing for maximal fetal development. In mice, the mother counteracts the pro-growth tumult by expressing a gene for a cellular receptor that regulates the growth hormone's effectiveness, decreasing the sensitivity to that hormone. Thrust and parry.

Once a baby is born, imprinted genes take a particularly bizarre turn. Certain paternally expressed genes help make kids active nursers. So that's another example of the usual picture: faster development at the cost of Mom's lactational calories. But now we're talking about imprinted genes that influence behavior. Other genes influence brain development in even stranger ways.*

The discovery of imprinted genes may pave the way for curing a number of diseases involving tumors, infertility, and fetal overgrowth or underdevelopment. But in addition, philosophically, the findings are disturbing and appear to have some deflating implications about human nature. Back to the logic of the Drosophila wars—what does the male care about the female's future? Ditto for imprinted genes among, say, hamsters, where nomadic males show up only for a quickie. But what about us? "In sickness and in health," we promise, "until death do us part." We're the species that came up with Paul Newman and Joanne Woodward. For monogamous animals, the future health and fertility of the female is as much in the male's interest as hers. So what are these imprinted genes doing in a human couple pondering which appetizers to serve at their golden wedding anniversary party?

The answer is that reports of our monogamy are greatly exaggerated. Features of human anatomy and physiology argue against it. Most human cultures allow polygamy. And most studies, ranging from genetic tests of paternity to a recent cover story in *Newsweek,* suggest that a lot of action is going on outside the pair-bond, even in monogamous societies. We have more in common with fruit flies than commonly believed. (Mind you, we're not one of the more polygamous species around. Even our busiest patriarchs weigh in with only a few hundred kids.) So much for our much-touted monogamy.

This can get demoralizing—Drosophila poisoning their lovers, maternally and paternally derived genes slugging it out in the fetus as

---

*Some maternally derived genes favor the fetus developing a bigger cortex, the intellectual part of the brain. Mutations that knock out those genes cause retardation. Meanwhile, some paternally expressed genes favor growth of the hypothalamus, which controls many unconscious body functions. How do these imprinted genes related to brain development and function fit into a framework of intersexual warfare? Speculations are rife, but no one is all that sure.

Mom and Dad choose a color scheme for the baby's room. Does nature have to be so bloody in tooth and claw and gene? Does everything have to be based on competition? Why can't we all just get along?

Here's where the evolutionary biologist, with Bogartesque weariness, pulls out the great cliché of his field. Biology isn't about what should be, he explains, but what is. It's a tough evolutionary world out there, it's dog outreproduce dog . . . certain things are inevitable.

But a subsequent study by Rice and Brett Holland hints that this need not be inevitable after all. With careful manipulation, it can be derailed. The researchers isolated pairs of mating flies, forcing them to be monogamous. They then bred their offspring only with the offspring of other such enforced monogamous pairs, continuing to maintain the monogamy. And after only forty generations, the monogamous descendants had disarmed—the males had stopped producing their sperm toxin, and the females had stopped producing the antitoxin. From the very first mating in which intermale competition was no longer a selective force, the rules had changed, it now being a maladaptive waste of energy to produce these chemicals. And as a bigger surprise, these monogamous flies *outbred* the usual competitive flies. Their approach was more evolutionarily fit, since they were freed of the expenditure of intersexual warfare. This is beautiful. John Lennon's "Imagine" soars in the background as we realize the implications: no Drosophila military budget and safe fly sex, a universe at peace in which no fly will be afraid.

Just picture carrying out the same experiment in people. Isolate some humans and force them and their descendants into monogamy for a millennium and we would probably begin to disarm our mammalian weapons of intersexual warfare, namely imprinted genes. These genes can be an evolutionary burden, making possible some truly horrendous cancers. Remove the advantages of these genes by eliminating polygamy, and natural selection should edit them out.

This is a truly weird place we've arrived at, should we care to do some moralizing—join the monogamy bandwagon, remember the Seventh Commandment, all as part of the "Let's Whip Choriocarcinoma by the Year 3000" campaign. Time to take a step back. Understanding how intersexual competition started with flies is relatively easy. Thanks to random genetic variability, some male flies would stumble into ever so slightly toxic sperm, which the females had to detoxify or die. And from there, the competition had spiraled upward. The start of imprinted genes is a bit more complicated, but once there was the first asymmetry of paternally derived genes pushing for the-hell-with-the-mom growth, the flip-flopping escalation had to begin. If the tribe next door shows up at the Paleolithic watering hole with clubs that seem just a wee bit on the big side for bonking animals over the head, the home team will naturally respond by getting even bigger clubs, just in case. And soon we have a world of choriocarcinoma, toxic fruit-fly semen, and umpteen times the education budget buying $600 toilet seats for the military. As in so many arenas of conflict, it's easier to ratchet up than down.

⟶ NOTES AND FURTHER READING ⟵

The shift away from "group selection" thinking and an introduction to the modern framework of thinking about the evolution of behavior are found in the magisterial (this is not a word I use often, but here it is deserved) Wilson EO, *Sociobiology, the Modern Synthesis* (Cambridge: Harvard University Press, 1975).

For a good introduction to intersexual competition in the context of evolution, see Miller M, *The Mating Mind: How Sexual Choice Shaped the Evolution of Human Nature* (New York: Doubleday, 2001). The notion that we humans are not quite the pair-bonding species that we like to think of ourselves as is the centerpiece of Barash D and Lipton J, *The Myth of Monogamy: Fidelity and Infidelity in Animals and People* (New York: Owl Books, 2002).

Rice's Drosophila work: Rice WR, "Sexually antagonistic male adaptation triggered by experimental arrest of female evolution," *Nature* 381 (1996): 232; Rice W, "Male fitness increases when females are eliminated from gene pool: implications for the Y chromosome," *Proceedings of the National Academy of Sciences, USA* 95 (1998): 6,217; and Holland B and Rice W, "Experimental removal of sexual selection reverses intersexual antagonistic coevolution and removes a reproductive load," *Proceedings of the National Academy of Sciences, USA* 96 (1999): 5,083.

Haig's work is reviewed in Wilkins J and Haig D, "What good is genomic imprinting: the function of parent-specific gene expression," *Nature Reviews Genetics* 4 (2003): 359.

For a review of imprinted genes relevant to brain development, see Keverne E, "Genomic imprinting in the brain," *Current Opinion in Neurobiology* 7 (1997): 463.

For the role of imprinted genes in postnatal growth, see Itier J et al., "Imprinted gene in postnatal growth role," *Nature* 393 (1998): 125.

The *Newsweek* cover story was "The New Infidelity" (July 12, 2004).

And for a phenomenally nutty, entertaining book, see Judson O, *Dr. Tatiana's Sex Advice to All Creation* (New York: Owl Books, 2003). The imaginary Dr. Tatiana writes an imaginary column of sex advice for animals of all sorts of species.

Of Mice and (Hu)Men Genes

Don't you love those urban legends, those outrageous stories that everyone believes? There are academicians who study urban legends for a living, catalog them, track their origins in Norse mythology, get into arguments at conferences about them. But amid all that intellectualizing, it's just plain fascinating to hear some of the stories that lots of people fall for. There's the endlessly repeated one about the person who puts the poodle in the microwave to dry it off, or the classic about the scuba diver who gets scooped up along with a lot of water into the giant bucket of a firefighting plane, then is dropped onto a forest fire. Then there's the one about the woman who leaves groceries in her car on a sweltering day; a tube of cookie dough explodes from the heat just as she gets in, splattering the back of her head, and she's convinced she's been shot and the dough is her splattered brains.

And then there's the one about a bunch of scientists who sequenced the human genome: they can explain everything about you; all they have to do is look it up in the sequence of your genes. Sure, someone has a cousin who has a friend whose uncle swears that he can explain everything since helping to sequence the human genome. But it just ain't so; we're back in the domain of urban legend.

Why are people such suckers for the idea that genes are the be-all and end-all? It's particularly bad right now. Not only has the human genome recently been (mostly) sequenced, but we've just come off the golden anniversary of the discovery of the structure of DNA. The celebrations have been replete with religious imagery about the genetic code as Holy Grail, the Code of Codes.

This Holy Grail business even gets trotted out by biologists, people who get paid to know better. This is surprising when it happens because, as emphasized in some of the preceding chapters, genes are not these autonomous instructors. Instead, we're back in the realm of gene/environment interactions, a phrase that is typically the first uttered by biologists in their infancy.

The idea that genes and environment interact can mean a number of things. At the least, it means that people who get into frenzied arguments about nature versus nurture are a century out-of-date. Of more relevance, it means that while genes can (indirectly) instruct cells, organs, and organisms as to how to function in the environment, the environment can regulate which genes are active at particular times—this was one of the main points of "A Gene for Nothing." Of greatest relevance here, it means that the thing that a particular gene most proximally produces—a particular protein—will function differently in different environments. So, in theory, you've got some gene that in one environment causes you to grow antlers, while in another, it causes you to fly south for the winter.

For folks still fighting the nature/nurture wars, the debate now becomes, Okay, just how powerful are those gene/environment interactions? At one extreme are those who scoff at antlers/fly-south contrasts. In that view, a gene does something or other, and environment can alter just how fast or strong or long it does that something or other. But none of those environmental influences leads to dramatically different effects. Framed in the context of genes and disease, it's like saying, yeah, how windy it is may alter the precise speed with which the anvil drops from a ten-story building and lands on your toe, but who cares about that environmental interaction with the anvil? And at the other extreme are those who assert that interactions can be of huge consequence—say, that an environmental factor like wind could result in an anvil dropping with the force of a feather.

And so the scientists happily argue and experiment away, squandering tax dollars that could otherwise go for Halliburton contracts. Amid these debates, it's useful to be reminded of just how powerful gene/environment interactions can be, and three recent studies provide great examples.

The first concerns the effects of one of the subtlest, least appreciated environments: the prenatal one. As was outlined in "Genetic Hyping," strains of laboratory rodents have been bred for various traits—this strain develops a type of diabetes, that strain gets hypertension, and so on. Each strain is developed by inbreeding generation after generation of animals with some trait, until all the members of the strain are close to being genetically identical—like clones of each other. If all the members of that strain show the trait, regardless of what lab they're raised in, you may have begun to detect a strong genetic influence (and, as the main point of essay three, even some of the genes most acclaimed at influencing behavior turn out not to have consistent effects across consistent environments).

All the inbreeding is then followed by a critical experiment known as a "cross-fostering study." Suppose all mice of Strain A grow up to prefer Coke to Pepsi, whereas the mice of Strain B always have the opposite opinion. Take some Strain A mice at birth and let Strain B moms raise them in a Strain B colony. If they still grow up craving Coke, the typical interpretation is that you've found a behavior that is strongly resistant to environment; score one for nature over nurture. But are cross-fostering studies the last word?

That's where this new study comes in, carried out by neurobiologist Darlene Francis and colleagues at Emory University, and published in the prestigious journal *Nature Neuroscience*. They looked at two mouse strains with differences in an array of behaviors. To simplify a bit, one strain is more anxious and skittish than the other. As compared with the "relaxed" strain, the "timid" strain is slower to enter a scary or novel environment and has more trouble learning during a stressful task than relaxed-strain mice do.

Geneticists who study mice had known about those differences for a long time. They had also confirmed that the differences were largely governed by genetics. True, some evidence showed that relaxed-strain mothers are more nurturing than timid-strain moms, licking and grooming their pups more. That evidence had raised the worrisome possibility for the gene crowd that mothering style caused the differences between the two strains. But then the acid test had been performed: relaxed-strain mice that were raised from birth by timid-strain moms grew up to be just as relaxed as any other member of their strain.

But Francis and team went a step further. With the same kind of technology used by clinics performing in vitro fertilization, the investigators cross-fostered mice as embryos. Specifically, they implanted fertilized relaxed-strain eggs into timid-strain females who carried them to term. They also did the key control of implanting "relaxed" eggs into "relaxed" females (just in case the in vitro fertilization and implantation distorted the results). After they were born, some relaxed-strain pups were raised by timid-strain moms, and others by relaxed-strain ones.

And the result? When the supposedly genetically hardwired "relaxed" mice went through both fetal development and early puphood with timid-strain moms, they grew up to be just as timid as any other timid-strain mice. Same genes, different environment, different outcome.

This raises two points. First, environmental influences don't begin at birth. Some factor or factors in the environment of a timid-strain mouse mother during her pregnancy—her level of stress, perhaps, or the nutrition she gets—are affecting the anxiety levels and learning abilities of her offspring, even as adults. The mechanisms may have to do with alterations in their brain structure, hormone profiles, or metabolism. In fact, some of the same prenatal effects have already been documented in people. The second point? Relaxed-strain mice aren't relaxed only because of their genes; their fetal and neonatal environments are crucial factors.

So that has to be a bit unnerving for folks who subscribe heavily to that urban legend about the power of genes. The next example makes the point even more strongly, mainly because, initially, it seems like one big vote for genetic determinism. This study was also published in *Nature Neuroscience* and was carried out by Joe Tsien and colleagues at Princeton, the folks who invented the "Doogie" mouse discussed in "Genetic Hyping." As you'll recall, Tsien and team generated the Doogie mouse by artificially inserting a gene that boosted the function of a particular class of neurotransmitters (the chemicals that carry messages between brain cells). And this produced a brilliant mouse that could do calculus and balance a checkbook. Now Tsien and crew generated a "knockout" mouse that lacked a key gene relevant to the neurotransmitter system, which coded for a receptor for that neurotransmitter. And thanks to some real wizardry, they were able to restrict this effect to only that one part of the brain critical to learning and memory—in terms of accuracy, this is the equivalent of a smart bomb from a hundred miles out taking out only the argyle socks in Saddam's clothes closet. As a result, everything about that neurotransmitter and its receptor was hunky-dory elsewhere in the brains of these mice, but this receptor system was completely knocked out of business in that one part of the brain.

The authors then demonstrated that these mice had all sorts of learning problems. They were lousy at recognizing objects, at making olfactory discriminations (something that rodents, not surprisingly, specialize in), at a certain type of contextual learning. These are all subtypes of memory that normally depend on that part of the brain. And, as one of the many of their excellent controls, the authors also showed that types of memory that don't involve that brain region worked just fine in these mice.

Wonderful, exciting. The authors have shown just how important those receptors are in that part of the brain for memory in these mice. And given that humans possess this same neurochemical system in their brains, there are immediately all sorts of implications that jump to mind. Different people have different versions of the gene for this receptor. Which might then result in the receptor working differently. Which might result, it now seems, in memory working differently. A defining feature of our individuality, traced down to the level of an individual gene. DNA City, nature trashing nurture, hands down.

Then the authors did something *really* interesting. There's a classic old paradigm in psychology in which you take baby rodents and, instead of raising them in boring, sterile cages, you put them into these stimulating environments, filled with running wheels and tunnels to burrow in, and great mouse toys. Remarkably, such "environmentally enriched" rodent pups develop into smarter animals, with better brain development, all sorts of good stuff. And environmental enrichment even does similarly good things to the brains of adult rodents, good news for all of us who are no longer young pups.

So Tsien and friends took some of these genetically dim mice and placed them, as adults, in an enriched environment. And, amazingly, it corrected some of those genetically based learning deficits. To reiterate, this isn't some subtle genetic alteration stacked up against some running wheels and squeeze toys. This was a massive genetic defect, the complete obliteration of a critical gene in a part of the brain vital to learning and memory. And the right sort of stimulating environment could correct it.

Findings like those that emerged from these two papers may give a panic attack to mouse mothers the world over: Remember the time we got all stressed out when we were pregnant? Remember that other time we got irritable with our newborn pup? One of them could be the reason the kid won't get into the best college. However, this topic might seem a bit far afield from human concerns. And this is where the final study comes in.

This landmark paper was published in *Science,* by Avshalom Caspi and colleagues at King's College, London. These researchers have been doing work that puts to shame those studies that come out of watching some fruit fly with a twenty-four-hour life span. They've been following a population of more than a thousand New Zealand kids, beginning in infancy and running well into adulthood, nigh onto a quarter century. Among the things they've examined is who, as a young adult, suffers from clinical depression. This is a useful topic to get some insight about, given that depression can be life threatening and afflicts 5 to 20 percent of us.

Caspi's team examined patterns of depression in their subjects and discovered that it has something to do with a variant of a gene. Now, that's nice, but not necessarily earth-shattering. Maybe the gene is involved with, say, how your ankle bones form. Hmm, its relevance to depression seems tenuous; maybe it's just a statistical red herring. Instead, the gene they implicated is at the center of biochemical theories about depression, coding for a protein that helps regulate how much serotonin gets into neurons. Serotonin is a neurotransmitter, one of scores of different kinds in the brain, but is the one responsive to antidepressant drugs like Prozac, Paxil, and Zoloft. The serotonin-regulating gene—which for reasons not worth going into is called 5-HTT—comes in two different flavors. Both flavors code for the same kind of protein, but they differ in how much of the protein gets produced, and how readily it regulates serotonin. Humans differ as to which version of 5-HTT our genes code for. Nonhuman primates do as well, and studies had already shown that a monkey's 5-HTT type influences how readily it deals with stress.

So Caspi and colleagues tabulated the two 5-HTT gene flavors and how they correlated with the incidence of depression in their pool of subjects. And what they discovered is worth stating carefully. Did they demonstrate that genes of a certain flavor cause depression? No. Did they even show something milder, that having one flavor of 5-HTT significantly increases the *risk* of depression? Not really.

What they showed was that if you have a particular flavor of 5-HTT, you have a greatly increased risk of depression, but *only in a certain environment.* What kind of environment? One with a history of major stressful events and traumas in childhood or early adulthood (such as the death of a loved one, the loss of a job, a serious illness). Those in their study with a "bad" 5-HTT profile who also suffered major stressful events had almost twice the risk of depression, and nearly four times the risk of suicide or suicidal thoughts, as those with the "best" profile plus an equivalent history of stress. But those who were spared a history of major stressors were no worse off for having a "bad" 5-HTT profile. (Completing this picture is work by a group at the University of Warburg, Germany, showing that stress hormones regulate the activity of the gene for 5-HTT, and do so differently depending on the 5-HTT flavor.)

So what does your 5-HTT variant have to do with your risk of depression? It's not even a valid question to ask. The only accurate way to approach the question is to ask what your 5-HTT variant has to do with your risk of depression in a particular environment.

What lessons lurk in these three studies? Obviously, beware of simple explanations; it is rare that nature is parsimonious. And keep genes in their proper place. Sometimes genetics is about inevitability—if you have the gene for Huntington's disease, for instance, there's a 100 percent chance you're going to have this awful neurological disease by middle age. But in far more realms than people usually expect, genes are about vulnerabilities and potentials, rather than about destiny.

And out of that comes a social imperative—genes do indeed seem to play a role in some of our less desirable behaviors. But what knowledge about those genes keeps teaching us is that we have that much more of a responsibility to create environments that interact benignly with those genes.

◦ NOTES AND FURTHER READING ◦

The study by Darlene Francis and colleagues is Francis D, Szegda K, Campbell G, Martin W, and Insel T, "Epigenetic sources of behavioral differences in mice," *Nature Neuroscience* 6 (2003): 445.

Prenatal environment has been shown to have lifelong effects on metabolism and risk of metabolic disease, reproductive function, brain development, and behavior in mammals, including humans. This is reviewed in Barker D and Hales C, "The thrifty phenotype hypothesis," *British Medical Bulletin* 60 (2001): 5; Gluckman P, "Nutrition, glucocorticoids, birth size, and adult disease," *Endocrinology* 142 (2001): 1,689; Dodic M, Peers A, Coghlan J, and Wintour M, "Can excess glucocorticoid, in utero, predispose to cardiovascular and metabolic disease in middle age?" *Trends in Endocrinology and Metabolism* 10 (1999): 86; Avishai-Eliner S, Brunson K, Sandman C, and Baram T, "Stressed-out, or in (utero)?" *Trends in Neuroscience* 25 (2002): 518; and Vallee M, Maccari S, Dellu F, Simon H, LeMoal M, and Mayo W, "Long-term effects of prenatal stress and postnatal handling on age-related glucocorticoid secretion and cognitive performance: a longitudinal study in the rat," *European Journal of Neuroscience* 11 (1999): 2,906.

The Tsien study regarding the cognitively impaired mouse rescued by environmental enrichment: Rampon C, Tang Y, Goodhouse J, Shimizu E, Kyin M, and Tsien J, "Enrichment induces structural changes and recovery from nonspatial memory deficits in CA1 NMDAR1-knockout mice," *Nature Neuroscience* 3 (2000): 238. This also contains references for general reviews on environmental enrichment.

The Caspi study on the "depression gene": Caspi A, Sugden K, Moffitt T, Taylor A, Craig I, Harrington H, McClay J, Mill J, Martin J, Braithwait A, and Poulton R, "Influence of life stress on depression: moderation by a polymorphism in the 5-HTT gene," *Science* 301 (2003): 386. For a similar finding in nonhuman primates: Bennett A,

Lesch K, Heils A, Long J, Lorenz J, Shoaf S, Champoux M, Suomi S, Linnoila M, and Higley J, "Early experience and serotonin transporter gene variation interact to influence primate CNS function," *Biological Psychiatry* 7 (2002): 118.

Regulation of 5-HTT by stress hormones: Glatz K, Mossner R, Heils A, and Lesch K, "Glucocorticoid-regulated human serotonin transporter (5-HTT) expression is modulated by the 5-HTT gene-promoter-linked polymorphic region," *Journal of Neurochemistry,* 86 (2003): 1,072.

The broad subject of the interactions between stress and depression is reviewed in chapter 14 in Sapolsky R, *Why Zebras Don't Get Ulcers: A Guide to Stress, Stress-Related Diseases, and Coping,* 3rd ed. (New York: Henry Holt, 2004).

Finally, for an encyclopedic (reasonably enough) overview of urban legends, see Brunvand J, *Encyclopedia of Urban Legends* (New York: Norton, 2002).

Antlers of Clay

For the many of you who are avid readers of both *Animal Behaviour* and *Cosmo,* it must be quite obvious that females the world over are concerned about finding the right mate. For females in pair-bonding species (such as swans, which mate for life, or monogamous South American monkeys), competency at fatherhood is a potential mate's most desirable quality. In many of these species, courting males display paternal skills: male lovebirds, for example, snatch worms and pretend to feed them to a desired female.

But selecting a good coparent is also high on the list for female *Homo sapiens*—a species that hardly rates as a textbook pair-bonder—namely us humans. About a decade ago, psychologist David Buss of the University of Texas at Austin published a celebrated study about what people look for in a mate. He canvassed more than ten thousand people from thirty-seven different cultures—people of different races, religions, and ethnicities; people living in urban and rural settings, Western and developing nations, capitalist and socialist economies, monogamous and polygamous family settings. And in every society Buss examined, he found that women were more likely than men to consider someone's economic prospects as a high priority in looking for a mate. This was interpreted as a sign that human females universally want mates who will be effective breadwinners. (As one might imagine, that generated all sorts of unsettling tremors of political incorrectness.)

And even in social species that don't pair off to reproduce, females often choose their mates based on how the male is likely to treat them or their offspring (a subject that will be covered in essay fifteen, "Monkeyluv"). For a female olive baboon, for example, a prize catch would be a male who, when in a foul mood, displaces aggression on some other female, rather than directing it at her.

But what about species where a female isn't going to be getting any paternalism out of the male she mates with, isn't even going to be having contact with him down the line? In such species, males are not integrated into social groups (the typical arrangement is a stable group of females with a single breeding male who is likely to be booted out by some other male long before his own young are born—a social structure typically called a harem by sociobiologists but which the primatologist Alison Jolly suggests should instead be called a gigolo group). All the female gets is some sperm packed with genes from the guy. What does such a female desire in a male? *Good* genes, of course.

Thus, the age-old problem for such females is how to figure out which males have those good genes, and in species after species males try to advertise those genes. Now we've entered the world of peacocks strutting in front of peahens, or males brandishing their elaborate manes or wild coloration or ornate antlers. In such species, these features can serve a number of purposes. They may aid in male-male combat. They may aid in attracting a mate because they signal that the male possesses a big, resource-rich territory, or because they tap into a sensory preference of the female's (for example, some male birds have probably evolved round, red plumage patches because females are attracted to red fruit). But in some cases, these ornamental features have evolved as a means for males to try to convince females that they carry good genes. And the question that has long vexed evolutionary biologists is whether these ornaments actually tell you anything about the genetic health of a male. In other words, is there truth in advertising?

In 1930, British statistician and geneticist Ronald Fisher, one of the most influential evolutionary thinkers of the past century, postulated that fancy ornamentation is actually something a female should *not* be attracted to, because huge energy expenditures to grow and maintain it would have a price tag in terms of the male's survival and evolutionary fitness. According to this view, if the guy has spent so much on growing the biggest whatsit around, he couldn't possibly have spent enough on something sensible, like keeping his immune system well tuned. While Fisher's view has generally fallen out of favor, some striking support for it has recently emerged. Robert Brooks and John Endler, of James Cook University in Australia, studied sexual attractiveness in male guppies of some species. They first showed that males with the fanciest color patterns were considered the most attractive by females and that they sired sons that were likely to be especially attractive. Color patterning, the scientists determined, is heritable and is sex-linked, coded for by a cluster of genes on the male's Y chromosome. Then Brooks and Endler found something that was enough of a surprise to get the paper published in *Nature*: sons of attractive males were significantly *less* likely to survive than average. And it isn't even the case that once they get this ornamentation, these males are more likely to be killed by a predator (a frequent cost of being flashy and conspicuous). Their survival rates were lower than average even *before* they reached sexual maturity and developed the coloration. So this experiment stands as one example in favor of the significant cost of attractive ornamentation.

Another view is that attractive decorations don't tell you much—good or bad—about the male's genes. Rather, they say something about fads. Jacob Hoglund and Arne Lundberg of Uppsala University in Sweden did an experiment that makes one appreciate this phenomenon. Pair up female and male black grouse that, tragically, have no chemistry—the female isn't interested in the male. Now use the wonders of modern science to turn him into a male who appears to be highly desirable—surround him with ostensibly rapt females (a gaggle of stuffed female birds)—and that test female suddenly decides he's kinda cute, after all. It's a bandwagon effect. This seems to mean that if all the females of your social group decide that males with paisley-pattern fur are really hot, even if you think it looks ridiculous, it is to your fitness advantage to want to mate with someone like that. After all, if paisley on males is suddenly all the rage, you want any sons you have to be paisley-patterned so that they can pass on as many copies of their genes as possible. By this circular logic, a trait becomes attractive because it's attractive because it's attractive . . . even if it is completely arbitrary and carries no information about the health or genes of the carrier.

Still another possibility is that attractive ornamentation really does translate into something meaningful and desirable about a male. Health may be the message: "You can bet I'm in good health if I can afford to waste all this energy growing these three-foot-long tail feathers." In 1982, Marlene Zuk and W. D. Hamilton, one of the gods of evolutionary biology, formalized this into the notion that conspicuous and expensive ornamentation in males signaled that they were free of parasites. Why should a female find that appealing? Because it decreases the likelihood that *she'll* wind up with some parasites after cozying up with the guy. If you're a species that reproduces sexually, you need to worry about sexually transmitted diseases.

But the more evolutionarily significant version of this theme is that attractive ornamentation not only signals good health, but good genes to be passed on to the next generation. Evolutionary biologist Amotz Zahavi of Tel Aviv University in Israel posits that females should have evolved to be able to differentiate between ornamentation that genuinely reflects good genes and the kind that instead suggests bad genes or merely an acquired trait. As a facetious example of this principle, this would explain why women might prefer six-foot-tall men over five-foot-six-inch guys wearing six-inch platform shoes.

Do things actually work this way? Does attractive ornamentation really indicate good genes? Theoretically, you could answer this in at least two ways. In the first version, you isolate the gene(s) responsible for the attractive trait in some males of some species. You then see what other genes are clustered nearby and that tend to be inherited with the attractiveness gene(s) in a statistically reliable way. You then figure out the function of the proteins coded for by those neighboring genes and whether these proteins are particularly advantageous. And soon you'll be in some zillion-dollar race to sequence the guppy genome.

Or you can do it the old-fashioned way. Carry out a study in which females are mated and have offspring with males of differing attractiveness. Then see whether the attractive guys father offspring who are more "fit"—more likely to survive to adulthood and to produce their own offspring. If they do, you've got a pretty good reason to conclude that the more attractive males pass on more adaptive assemblages of genes. And that is exactly what a number of studies have shown, casting a big vote in favor of the good-gene hypothesis.

Yet some startling revisionism has recently crept into that hypothesis. One example is a study of ducks, done by Emma Cunningham and Andrew Russell, then of Sheffield University in the UK, and published in *Nature*. They found that the offspring of male mallards that were particularly attractive to females have a trait that considerably increases their likelihood of survival. So more votes for the good-gene hypothesis. What was that trait? When females mated with the more attractive males, they laid large eggs, which definitely increases the fitness of the offspring. But wait—egg size is a trait determined by the *female,* not the male. When females mated with more attractive males, they invested more energy in the pregnancy, making the offspring more likely to survive. When Cunningham and Russell controlled for egg size, there was no survival difference between the offspring of the most and least attractive males.

In a similar study published in *Science,* Diego Gil and colleagues at the University of St. Andrews in Scotland studied zebra finches and found that the offspring of the more attractive males begged for more food, grew faster, and were more likely to be dominant once they fledged. Again, where is this coming from? The scientists found that when females mated with the more attractive males, they developed eggs that contained more growth-stimulating hormone. And then there's work by Felix de Lope of the University of Extremadura in Spain, and Anders Moller of University Pierre et Marie Curie in France, showing that when female barn swallows mate with more attractive males, they take better care of the resulting chicks.

All of this is actually a logical extension of the bandwagon effect uncovered by Hoglund and Lundberg. For starters, if everyone in your species "wants" to mate with males that have some trait that doesn't necessarily seem attractive to you, it's still in your best genetic interest to mate with these males, so that your sons have the desirable trait. And if everyone in your species "knows" that more attractive males make for offspring that carry better genes, and if you've mated with an attractive male, it's in your best genetic interest to invest as much as possible in the well-being of those offspring.

(A challenge is to figure out how a female knows she has mated with a more attractive male and how this translates into the differential investment in her young. How does that "knowledge"—on whatever level it exists in the brain of a bird—translate into synthesizing more growth hormone in a gland or going the extra mile to find the offspring something to eat? This remains a mystery.)

Studies of egg size, the amount of growth hormone in eggs, and parental investment generate serious problems for the good-looks/good-genes hypothesis. When Cunningham and Russell found that females with attractive mates grew bigger eggs, at first it raised the possibility that the underlying logic was "Everyone knows that more attractive males make kids with better genes, so I have to make sure these kids survive." But the researchers then found that the father's attractiveness had no effect on hatching success, survival, or growth. Maybe good genes really don't exist.

Findings such as Cunningham's and Russell's do not disprove the theory that more attractive males have better genes; quite possibly they do, most of the time. But these findings have uncovered a major alternative explanation for what has been observed—one that must now be ruled out in every subsequent study on the subject: If the offspring of attractive males are more fit, is it because the female has invested more energy in their survival?

So lots more research is needed, both to see how much the parental investment factor confounds the supposed cases of good genes and to understand the physiology behind females' differential investment in offspring and how this relates to the attractiveness of the father. In the meantime, this is exasperating. It's bad enough that males with longer tail feathers get more action, but they also get acclaimed for having better genes when this may not actually be the case. How fair is that?

This self-fulfilling-prophecy business runs through all sorts of settings. Everyone "knows" that boys are biologically better at math than girls are, so, studies have shown, young boys are more likely to be praised than girls by teachers for the same math performance. And what do you know, by high school, males score better on standardized math tests than girls. Due to a biological difference or the differential environment? Here's another example that has always amused me (it's from the medical anthropology literature): In certain traditional cultures, everyone "knows" that shamans are able to induce voodoo death (also known as psychophysiological death). So when someone has a voodoo hex put on him, everyone knows he's a goner, and they withhold food from him—why waste a limited resource?—to the point of his weakening and dying from one ailment or another. Death due to the efficacy of a voodoo curse or to this additional intervention? Not clear, but you can bet the shaman's hexing fees go up.

One sees such confusions popping up in all sorts of realms of human illogic. I'm just disappointed to see female mallards and zebra finches falling for something this obvious. They should know better than that.

⤙ NOTES AND FURTHER READING ⤚

For an excellent introduction to the fact that, from a biological standpoint, we humans are probably not all that monogamous, see Barash D and Lipton J, *The Myth of Monogamy: Fidelity and Infidelity in Animals and People* (New York: Owl Books, 2002).

David Buss's famed study is found in Buss D, *The Evolution of Desire: Strategies of Human Mating* (New York: Basic Books, 1994).

Fisher's (and Zahavi's) thinking are reviewed in Eshel I, Sansone E, and Jacobs F, "A long-term genetic model for the evolution of sexual preference: the theories of Fisher and Zahavi re-examined," *Journal of Mathematical Biology* 45 (2002): 1.

The Brooks study: Brooks R, "Negative genetic correlation between male sexual attractiveness and survival," *Nature* 406 (2000): 67.

The work by Hoglund and Lundberg is described in Dugatkin L and Godin J, "How females choose their mates," *Scientific American,* April 1998, 56.

The Hamilton/Zuk hypothesis was presented in Hamilton W and Zuk M, "Heritable true fitness and bright birds: a role for parasites?" *Science* 218 (1982): 384.

Zahavi's ideas are presented in Zahavi A, "Mate selection—a selection for a handicap," *Journal of Theoretical Biology* 53 (1975): 205.

Females changing the size of their eggs: Cunningham E and Russell A, "Egg investment is influenced by male attractiveness in the mallard," *Nature* 404 (2000): 74. Females altering the amount of testosterone in their offspring: Gil D, Graves J, Hazon N, and Wells A, "Male attractiveness and differential testosterone investment in zebra finch eggs," *Science* 286 (1999): 126. Females altering parental investment as a function of the attractiveness of the father: de Lope F and Moller A, "Female reproductive effort depends on the degree of ornamentation of their mates," *Evolution* 47 (1993): 1,152.

PART II

Our Bodies and Who We Are

Introduction

Task 1: Time for a small exercise. Take a few minutes to relax right now. Lean back in your chair, clear your mind of your endless cares and stressors, breathe deeply, hold it a second, then exhale slowly. Do it again a few times. Feel those muscles relax, feel the tension drain from your face, feel your heart begin to beat more slowly. Now, quick, think the following thought:

You know, someday that heart is going to stop beating.

Don't stop there. Really *think* about that fact, think about how every heartbeat is counting down toward that final one. Think about how the flow of blood will come to a standstill, how your brain will shut down for lack of oxygen. Think of your toes and fingers turning blue.

Now think about what thinking about this *feels* like. If you're like me, your heart is now racing, and there's this weird, icy panic clutching from your stomach down to your crotch, and your throat is sort of constricted in a way that makes you want to whimper or puke.

And thus you will have learned the first of two points that are critical to this part of the book: sometimes, all you need to do is think a thought and you change the functioning of virtually every cell in your body.

*　　*　　*

Task 2: Next, consider the following three things:
- Having a menstrual period.
- Taking anabolic steroids (these are the testosterone-related male sex steroids often abused by weight lifters).
- Eating too much junk food.

Now, what do they have in common?

You grope for an answer. They, er, all have something to do with biology. Well, yes, that's a pretty safe guess. They all have something to do with behavior or emotions or emotional behavior, or something like that. Getting warmer.

Give up? Each has been proffered in a court of law by defense attorneys as an explanation for a violent crime.* And thus we learn the second of the two critical points in this third of the book: sometimes, all you need to do is change events in the body—change the levels of some hormone, some nutrient, some immune factor—and you will change how your brain thinks and emotes.

This intertwining of our brains and bodies, their mutual capacity to regulate each other, is now a central concept of modern biology. Few dualists are out there anymore, for whom our mindness floats pristinely above all that nuts-and-bolts biology of cells and organelles and molecules. We are the product of those cells et al., and our brains are as fundamentally biological organs as are, say, our bladders—some muscle cell from the wall of your bladder, and some fancy turbocharged neuron from your cortex, have a lot more in common with each other than they have different. The brain is just another organ,

*For all but San Franciscans, the junk-food explanation is probably the most obscure. In late November 1978, Dan White, a disappointed office seeker and political malcontent, murdered George Moscone and Harvey Milk, respectively the mayor and the city supervisor/gay political icon of San Francisco. Among the defenses offered at his trial was the notion that a drastic change in blood sugar due to White's junk-food consumption (i.e., the notorious "Twinkie Defense") impaired his volitional control over his behavior. Though convicted of the murders, White was generally viewed as having received an appallingly short sentence.

albeit a fancy one, and its functioning is inseparable from its existence within the body. As the neurologist Antonio Damasio has put it, "The mind is embodied . . . not just embrained."

The ways in which the brain alters function throughout the body are numerous. There's the obvious way in which your brain, via the "voluntary nervous system," sends commands to your skeletal muscles. And suddenly your body shakes hands or signs a check or does the Bunny Hop.

Then there's the involuntary nervous system (also known as the autonomic nervous system), by which your brain regulates your body in ways over which you don't normally have much conscious control. And thus you blush or feel aroused or have an array of "autonomic responses" when you contemplate your inevitable mortality. Those cables of neurons from your brain that form the autonomic nervous system are turning out to project to all sorts of unexpected places. Some course from your spine to your bones, those most static and phlegmatic of outposts in the body, and influence what turns out to be the manic process of bone remodeling. Others project individually to each of millions of tiny, vestigial hair follicles in our limbs—and thus we are capable of getting gooseflesh. Others project to our immune organs, a basis of an entirely new scientific discipline, psychoneuroimmunology, the study of the ways in which the brain can regulate our immune defenses.

And then there's the ability of the brain to regulate the body through the secretion hormones. The brain turns out to be an endocrine gland, the master gland (a title that *Reader's Digest*-style science circa 1950 used to award to the pituitary), releasing scads of hormones that in turn direct the function of endocrine glands throughout the rest of the body.

And consider the other half of this brain/body circle of interactions, how events in your body can influence the brain. This has been known for a long time: thousands of years ago, someone carried out what was probably the first experiment in psychoneuroendocrinology, castrating a bull, thereby demonstrating that something or other emanating from the testes has something to do with male surliness. A long-standing belief was that parts of the brain were relatively unaffected by events in the body. This privileged domain, in this view, was the cortex, the most "cerebral" part of the brain. Sure, the brain regions that specialized in emotion were pickled in hormones, but the cortex was viewed as this gleaming, stainless-steel, affectless realm, half-calculator and half–objective philosopher king. This dichotomizing between emotion and cognition (and between the brain regions responsible for each) turns out to be completely false, a misconception termed "Descarte's error" by Damasio (in a superb book by the same name).

Instead, events in the body influence every aspect of brain function. The type and levels of sex hormones in your bloodstream will alter whether your brain is better at picking up the local details or the global features of a pattern. Chemical messengers released by your immune system will increase your risk of depression. Stress hormones will alter the functioning of a key outpost of your brain, the frontal cortex, and the prudence of the decisions that you make. In the aftermath of a trauma, your blood pressure, along with other autonomic measures, influences the likelihood of your succumbing to post-traumatic stress disorder. And even something as mundane as your blood sugar levels will alter how readily you remember some factoid.

The varied ways in which the brain and body interact, and the ways in which the brain is ultimately a mere biological organ, are the subjects of the essays in this part of the book. Essay seven, "Why Are Dreams Dreamlike?" introduces that critical part of the brain, the frontal cortex, and considers how in every one of us it is completely dysfunctional, shut down, and out of business, many times each day. Essay nine, "The Pleasure (and Pain) of 'Maybe,'" continues the theme of the frontal cortex, examining what it has to do with discipline and gratification postponement.

Essay eight, "Anatomy of a Bad Mood," and essay ten, "Stress and

Your Shrinking Brain," focus on how the body influences the brain. The first examines how your autonomic nervous system can make you do stupid things in your relationships, can make your brain decide that its feelings are deeply, sincerely hurt about something when it just isn't so. Essay ten takes a more tragic focus, examining how a class of hormones released during stress just might be damaging an area of the brain in people with certain types of post-traumatic stress disorder. This finding may turn out to be of ghastly relevance to the huge numbers of people seared by the events of 9/11.

Essay eleven, "Bugs in the Brain," examines a truly bizarre example of how the brain can be influenced by the world outside it. In this case, the brain's function is not being influenced by some hormone or nutrient in the bloodstream. Instead, some facets of its function are being controlled by parasites that get into the brain. Creepy stuff.

Essay twelve, "Nursery Crimes," examines a brain that is profoundly, grotesquely diseased and produces disease in the vulnerable body of someone else.

Why Are Dreams Dreamlike?

You find yourself at a banquet table. You feel disaffected because the people surrounding you are speaking a language you do not understand. Suddenly, you feel pressure on your foot—beneath the table, someone's foot is on your own. You glance up. Your eyes meet those of the attractive person sitting opposite you. Intuitively, you sense the word that you must now say to captivate this person. You say it: "Phlegm." The person stands, and suddenly the other people are gone. As is the table. As are your clothes. You fling yourselves at each other in passion. It is wondrous. The two of you are far up in the air, the sensuality of the experience heightened by the clouds brushing past you. Yet suddenly you begin to sob in shame, because you have been observed by your four deceased grandparents, who disapprove. You realize that the severe-looking man in the black frock coat comforting your maternal grandmother is William Seward, and with great clarity and an inexplicable sense of nostalgia, you recite, "William Henry Seward. U.S. secretary of state in the Andrew Johnson administration."

You know, one of *those* dreams.

Just as the kidney is a kidney-shaped organ, dreams are dreamlike. But why should that be? In real life you wouldn't wind up floating amid the clouds with someone seconds after the touch of a foot. Instead, at a key moment, you'd decide that he or she was actually kind of neurotic or note the bit of spinach stuck in his or her teeth or suddenly remember you'd forgotten to turn off the lights of your car. Dreams, by contrast, are characterized not only by rapid transitions but by a heightened sense of emotionality. Then there's the disinhibition: not only do you do things that you couldn't bring yourself to do in real life, but with two seconds of sensible reflection, you wouldn't remotely *want* to do them.

There has never been a shortage of theories as to the utility of dreams being dreamlike. Maybe dreaming is the channel by which the gods speak to mortals. Or maybe this is a good way to work out how you really feel about your mother without all that repression getting in the way. Maybe it's a way to get your brain to work in an unconventional, orthogonal manner to solve that pesky math problem you went to sleep thinking about. Or maybe this is how you keep underutilized neural pathways active (this theory has floated around for a while—if you spend all day long exercising those rational, sensible pathways in your brain, you need dreams to give an aerobic workout to those gibberish neurons, lest they shrivel up from disuse). Or maybe it's so you can have a sex dream about some unlikely person at work and then act all weird and knowing around them the next day at the water cooler. Or maybe the dreaming evolved so that the surrealists and dadaists could make a living.

How does your brain bring about this state of disinhibited imagery? Until recently, scientists understood little about the actual nuts and bolts of dreaming. But we've known for some time that sleep has a structure, an architecture, if you will, with rhythmic cycles during the night of deep, "slow-wave" sleep, interspersed with the REM (rapid eye movement) sleep, most associated with dreaming. And the levels of activity in the brain are not uniform throughout the stages of sleep. Techniques that indicate the overall levels of electrical excitability and activity in the brain have uncovered something pretty intuitively obvious: during deep, slow-wave sleep, the average level of brain activity goes way down. This fits well with studies suggesting that the main purpose of slow-wave sleep is to allow for the replenishing of energy stores in the brain—the proverbial recharging of the batteries. But something very different happens during the onset of dreaming during REM sleep—a big increase in electrical activity. And this has a certain intuitive logic to it as well.

Advances in brain-imaging technology now allow scientists to study activity and metabolism in the small subregions of the brain, rather than just in the brain as a whole. In a series of studies, Allen Braun and colleagues at the National Institutes of Health have examined the neuroanatomy of metabolism during sleep. I think they may have uncovered the explanation for why dreams are so dreamlike.

The researchers utilized positron-emission tomography (PET) to measure the various rates of blood flow throughout the brain. One of the remarkably adaptive features of the brain is that blood flow in a particular region will increase when that area increases its level of activity. In other words, there is a coupling between demand for energy and the supply of it. Thus, the extent of blood flow in an area of the brain can be used as an indirect index of the activity there. That is why PET scans, which show blood flow, are so helpful in this type of research.

Braun and crew got some volunteers who allowed themselves to be sleep-deprived for an ungodly twenty-four to fifty-three hours. Each bleary volunteer was then rolled into a PET scanner and forced to stay awake even longer, while a baseline PET scan was made. Then, snug as a bug inside the scanner, each subject was finally allowed to sleep, with the scanning continuing.

As the subjects slid into slow-wave sleep, the blood-flow changes observed made a lot of sense. Parts of the brain associated with arousal, known as the reticular activating system, shut down; ditto for brain regions involved in controlling muscle movement. Interestingly, regions involved in the consolidation and retrieval of memories did not have much of a decrease in blood flow, and hence metabolism. However, the pathways that brought information to and from those regions shut down dramatically, isolating them metabolically. The parts of the brain that first respond to sensory information had somewhat of a metabolic shutdown, but the more dramatic changes were in downstream brain areas that integrate and associate those bytes of sensory information, that give them meaning. The result: metabolically quiescent, sleeping brains.

While the scientists at the scanner's console bided their time, eventually the sleeping subjects transitioned into REM sleep. And then the picture changed. Metabolic rates leapt upward throughout regions of the brain. Cortical and subcortical regions that regulate muscle movement, brain-stem regions that control breathing and heart rate, all showed increases. A part of the brain called the limbic system, which is involved in emotion, showed an increase as well. The same for areas involved in memory and sensory processing, especially those involved in vision and hearing.

Meanwhile, something particularly subtle went on in the visual processing regions. The primary visual cortical region did not show much of an increase in metabolism, whereas there was a big jump in the downstream regions that integrate simple visual information. The primary visual cortical region is involved in the first steps of processing sight—the changing of patterns of pixels of light and dark into things like lines or curves. In contrast, the downstream areas are the integrators that turn those lines and curves into the perception of objects, faces, scenes. Normally, an increase in activity in the downstream areas cannot occur without an increase in those primary processing areas. In other words, when you're wide awake, you can't get from the eyes to complex pictures without going first through the initial level of analysis. But REM is a special case, where you're not using the eyes. Instead, you're starting with the downstream integration of visual patterns. This, Braun and colleagues speculated convincingly, is what makes up the imagery of dreams.

So there are increases in metabolism during REM sleep in numerous parts of the brain. In some regions, metabolic rates even wind up being considerably higher than during wakefulness. Now it's time for the exception that I think is the punch line about the dreaminess of dreams, in a region of the brain called the prefrontal cortex. Outside the prefrontal cortex, all of the brain regions most closely associated with the limbic system showed an increase in metabolism with the onset of REM sleep. But in the prefrontal cortex, only one of the four subregions increased. The rest of that area stayed on the floor of metabolic inactivity that it had sunk to during slow-wave sleep. This is interesting, given the functions of the prefrontal cortex. The human brain, when compared with your off-the-rack mammalian brain, has many unique features. Its sensory inputs and motoric outputs are uniquely fine-tuned to make it possible to whip off an arpeggio on a piano. The limbic system allows for something virtually unprecedented among mammals: sexual receptivity among females throughout the reproductive cycle, rather than merely at the time of ovulation. The vast cortex creates symphonies and calculus and philosophy, while the atypically numerous interconnections between the cortex and the limbic system allow for that dreadful human attribute, the ability to think oneself into a depression.

Yet in many ways, the most unique feature of the human brain is the extent of the development of, the power of, that prefrontal cortex—the region staying metabolically inhibited during REM sleep. The prefrontal cortex plays a central role in self-discipline, in gratification postponement, in putting a rein on one's impulses. On the facetious level, this is the part of the brain that keeps you from belching loudly in the middle of a wedding ceremony. On a more profound level, it keeps the angry thought from being allowed to become the hurtful word, the violent fantasy from becoming the unspeakable act.

Not surprisingly, other species don't have a whole lot of prefrontal function. Nor do young kids; the prefrontal cortex is basically the last part of the brain to fully mature, not coming completely online for decades. Violent sociopaths appear to have insufficient metabolic activity in the prefrontal region. And damage to the prefrontal cortex, such as after certain types of strokes, causes a disinhibited, "frontal" personality. The person may become apathetic or childishly silly, hypersexual or bellicose as hell, scatological or blasphemous.

Braun and colleagues found that during REM sleep, much of the prefrontal cortex was off-line, unable to carry out its waking task of censoring material, while the complex sensory-processing parts of the brain concerned with emotion and memories were highly active.

So bring on those dreams, now free to be filled with disinhibited actions and labile emotions. You breathe underwater, fly in the air, communicate telepathically; you announce your love to strangers, invent languages, rule kingdoms; you even star in a Busby Berkeley musical.

Mind you, even if it turns out that the inhibition of prefrontal metabolism during REM sleep explains the disinhibition of dream content, it still doesn't tell us anything about *why* some people's brains would want to spend some REM time in a Busby Berkeley musical. The specific content of dreams remains a mystery. Moreover, if true, this speculation would constitute one of the classic features of science—in explaining something, you've merely redefined the unknown. If the answer to the question "Why is dream content so disinhibited?" turns out to be "Because prefrontal cortical regions are atypically inactive during REM sleep," the new question obviously becomes "Then why are prefrontal cortical regions atypically inactive?"

Just as with anything else that can be studied and measured in living systems, the level of activity of the prefrontal cortex varies considerably in different individuals. As noted, there seem to be decreased metabolic rates in prefrontal regions in sociopaths. At the other end of the spectrum, Richard Davidson and colleagues at the University of Wisconsin have observed elevated prefrontal metabolic rates in people with "repressive personalities." These are highly controlled folks with superegos going full throttle, working overtime to keep their psychic sphincters good and tight. They dislike novelty, prefer structure and predictability, are poor at expressing emotions or at reading the nuances of emotions in other people. These are the folks who can tell you what they're having for dinner two weeks from Thursday.

This leads me to an idea that seems to flow naturally from the findings of Braun and his colleagues. The data regarding the sociopath/repressive continuum come from studies of awake individuals. Most certainly, there will also be considerable variability among people in prefrontal cortex functioning during REM sleep. While prefrontal metabolism may generally remain on the floor with the transition into REM sleep, there'll be exceptions. So I suspect it's likely that the more prefrontal metabolism remains suppressed during REM, the more vivid and disinhibited dream content will be. Better yet would be some comparative studies of prefrontal metabolism during wake and sleep. Do people who have the most active prefrontal cortices when awake have the least active when asleep? This would certainly fit the old hydraulic models of psychoanalysis, where if you repress something important during the day, it'll come oozing out during dreams.

I've occasionally heard med students come up with a witticism to express their typical disdain for classes in psychiatry: "What classes are you taking this semester?" "Oh, pathology, microbio, pharmacology, and this required seminar in laser psychotherapy." The last is meant to be an eccentric oxymoron. Laser-something-or-other equals high tech, as opposed to psychotherapy, as the pejoratively low-tech art of talk therapy. Thus, the student is saying, "They're forcing us to take some class with these shrinks who are trying to dress up their stuff as modern science." Wouldn't it be ironic if some reductive support for the seemingly antiquated Freudian concept of repression were to emerge from the bowels of a gazillion-dollar brain scanner?

─◦ NOTES AND FURTHER READING ◦─

For a nontechnical introduction to the neurobiology of sleep, see chapter 11 in Sapolsky R, *Why Zebras Don't Get Ulcers: A Guide to*

Stress, Stress-Related Diseases, and Coping, 3rd ed. (New York: Henry Holt, 2004).

Braun's work is reported in Braun A, Balkin T, Wesensten N, Gwadry F, Carson R, Varga M, Baldwin P, Belenky G, and Herscovitch P, "Dissociated patterns of activity in visual cortices and their projections during human rapid eye movement sleep," *Science* 279 (1998): 91.

The late maturation of the frontal cortex is documented in Paus T, Zijdenbos A, Worsley K, Collins D, Blumenthal J, Giedd J, Rapoport J, and Evans A, "Structural maturation of neural pathways in children and adolescents: in vivo study," *Science* 283 (1999): 1908. The function of the frontal cortex also figures in essay nine, "The Pleasure (and Pain) of 'Maybe'."

Anatomy of a Bad Mood

(Given that this was originally published in *Men's Health* magazine, the targeted "you" in the piece is a heterosexual male. Gen-
eralize beyond that as needed.)

Here's how it happens. You've done something piggish to your
significant other, something stupid and selfish and insensitive.
She's pissed. So you argue. And you make things worse initially by trying to defend yourself.

Somewhere amid the heated exchange, you actually think about
what you've done, consider it from her perspective, and realize, *Jeez,
I was a total jerk.* You apologize. You make it sound as if you sincerely
mean it. You actually do sincerely mean it.

She accepts your apology, does a "But don't ever do that again"
parting shot with a flair of the nostrils. You start to feel pretty
pleased with yourself; got off easy this time, you realize. That flair of
her nostrils has even made you think about sex. You eye the bedroom.
Phew, sure glad that's over with.

And then she suddenly dredges up some argument the two of you
had about some other jerky thing you did years ago, the time you forgot to do X, or the time she caught you doing Y. It has *nothing* to do
with the jerky thing you just did. You barely remember it. But she
remembers every detail and is raring to go over it again in all its minu-
tiae, just when the tension was dissipating.

What's up with this? (And why have you done the same on occasion?) It's not because she's unconsciously trying to torpedo the relationship, or because she gets some obscure pleasure from fighting. It is simply that her limbic and autonomic nervous systems operate at different speeds.

Whah?

It all has to do with the psychologist/philosopher William James. Yes, your personal life is about to be improved by the insights of some nineteenth-century dead white male who gets university buildings named after him. James speculated about how the brain decides what kind of emotion we're feeling. Something happens, your brain figures out its emotional response—anger, elation, arousal, terror, whatever. Then your brain tells your body how to respond—your heart races, you breathe faster, you get gooseflesh, you get an erection, whatever. These responses are controlled by something called the autonomic nervous system, which, as discussed earlier in the introduction to this third of the book, is involved in things that are automatic (that is, autonomic) throughout your body.

Makes sense. But James came up with a nutty idea that reverses the direction of all this. He believed that your body's autonomic response, not your brain, determines the emotion you think.

In James's view, your brain assesses the situation too quickly for you to be consciously aware yet of what you are feeling about it and rapidly kicks your body into gear with whatever autonomic response it is going to have. Your brain then canvasses your body to see how it's reacting to the outside stimulus. So conscious emotions don't shape your autonomic bodily response; your autonomic bodily response shapes the conscious emotion you feel.

Weird; seems ass backward, and it did to a lot of James's contemporaries. But his ideas are turning out to be true in a lot of ways. Your autonomic nervous system may not quite determine the exact type of emotion you're feeling, but it has tons to do with emotional intensity.

There's all sorts of evidence for this by now. Studies on quadriplegics—people who are not only paralyzed but also get no tactile feeling from their body—show a strong blunting of emotion. The same goes for people with diseases that affect the autonomic nervous system. They have normal tactile sensations and experience pleasure, anger, and fear like anyone else. They just have no involuntary bodily responses to those emotions. If they're afraid, for example, their hearts don't race, their skins don't get clammy. If saddened, they don't cry. If angered, their muscles don't tense up. And they feel less emotion than normal.

Experimental manipulations show this as well. If you force someone to make a certain emotionally strong facial expression over and over, he'll start to feel an emotion that agrees with the expression. For example, depressed people who are asked to repeatedly make big, booming smiles usually begin to feel better. In an experiment done years ago before there were laws against this sort of thing, researchers secretly injected volunteers with adrenaline, the main hormone that mediates emotional arousal throughout the body. What happened? They experienced more intense emotions. When some of the subjects went into a waiting room with someone (secretly part of the experiment) who acted extroverted and gregarious, the adrenaline-juiced subjects became much more outgoing than did volunteers who were injected with only saline. When the adrenaline-injected subjects entered a room with an angry, abrasive person, they too became angrier than the control subjects did.

Perhaps the clearest example of James's theory in action comes from one of the most common drugs prescribed, one used to control emotions. Suppose you are worried all the time—can't sleep, can't concentrate. A physician might prescribe an antianxiety drug for you, a minor tranquilizer. Meanwhile, across town, some jock who has gotten an injury just before an important game is getting these miserable muscle spasms. A physician might prescribe a muscle-relaxant drug. And amazingly, the muscle relaxant and the antianxiety drug are the same exact medication (something like Valium or Librium).

Why does the same drug work for both problems? Because, à la William James, your brain is telling you you're bat-shit crazy anxious because your tense muscles are telling that to your brain. Take some Valium, which works, most directly, to decrease muscle tension. Wait a few hours. Your life will still be just as awful as it was two hours ago—but thanks to that muscle relaxant, your body is so loose that you can barely even sit up straight. And somehow, you conclude, *Well, if I feel like I'm like Jell-O . . . maybe things aren't so bad after all.* And you feel less anxious.

So, hooray for Professor James; the intensity of the emotions you feel is shaped by what autonomic events are going on in your body at the time. But what's this have to do with your girlfriend raking you over the coals for something that happened years ago, when it seemed your fight was over?

The key is the differing speeds with which your brain and the rest of your body operate. Suppose you're walking in a crowd. Someone bumps into you from behind, really hard, bashes into your instep. *Asshole,* you think, turning to snarl at them. You see the dark glasses and cane—*Oh, he's blind, that's why he bumped into me, not a big deal.* A thought turned on and off in two seconds.

Another example: You're playing racquetball, and your thoughts are changing many times a second—*Move to the left; he's going to angle it; no, he's not; reach out far; twist it to the corner.* Your emotional evaluations, something controlled by a part of the brain called the limbic system, are changing at that sort of speed as well—*Man, I'm playing well; damn, he's going to blast it past me; I stink; wow, amazing, I'm totally awesome at this; argh, no, I'm not . . .*

Your limbic system moves and switches gears almost instantly. But, critically, the autonomic parts of your body move like a freight train; they build speed gradually and take a long time to come to a stop. Adrenaline is secreted, your heart speeds up, your sweat glands get activated. And after the thoughts that prompted these changes have come and gone, it takes a while for adrenaline to clear from your bloodstream, for your heart to slow down, and so on.

So you've done that jerky thing, and she's pissed. This is a cognitive event for her—her cortex is thinking, *This was not appropriate behavior on his part.* This is an emotional event for her—her limbic system is ruminating, *He's a jerk and I'd like to strangle him.* Pretty quickly, this also turns into a bodily event for her as her autonomic nervous system triggers her heart to race and her muscles to clench in fury.

Finally, you apologize. And, as a cognitive event, it's over with. The neuronal pathways involved can reverse pretty quickly. But the bodily responses are still chugging along. And here the ghost of William James comes to ruin the scene you had in mind as a result of that hot nostril flair. She *knows* that it is resolved—you apologized. But if that heart is still racing, if all the other autonomic baggage is still going like crazy, it doesn't yet *feel* as if it's resolved. And the mind fills an explanatory vacuum: *Well, I know he apologized, but since I still feel agitated, there must be something else that I'm upset about. Ah, I know, it's that insensitive thing he did three years ago . . . what a jerk.* And she's off and running.

Naturally, there's a sex difference to make things worse. Consider sexual arousal, which is also regulated by the autonomic nervous system: on average, men get aroused faster than women, and when it is all over with, women stay aroused longer, which explains why afterward she wants to hear you say whispery things, when all you want is to find a place that delivers Chinese food this time of night. And while it's not as well studied, it appears as if under all kinds of nonsexual circumstances, the autonomic nervous system recovers back to baseline more quickly in men than women. So while men are perfectly capable of doing the "Just when we thought the fight was over with, out comes the pointless rehashing of some event from decades ago," women are probably more likely to.

So what do you do about this? How are we going to market the *William James Self-Help Relationship Guide*? Obvious. Try to counteract that locomotive of an autonomic nervous system with a mind of its own. How to do it? Obviously not so easy. Well, there are all sorts of clunky time-out tricks to try: before you can answer, you have to take a deep breath or stop and count to ten. Make a rule that you must argue sitting down (this will slow down the flow of adrenaline). Or use cognition as ammunition: discuss this autonomic arousal business with her so you can both short-circuit the phenomenon: "Hey, are we having a William James moment here?"

Relationships can be contentious enough without your glands suckering you into inventing problems that don't exist.

⁓ NOTES AND FURTHER READING ⁓

William James and his ideas run through any introductory psychology textbook, while the workings of the autonomic nervous system run through any introductory physiology text. The role of autonomic arousal in maintaining cognitive arousal was discussed (in the context of aggression) in Zillmann D, "Cognition-excitation interdependencies in aggressive behavior," *Aggressive Behavior* 14 (1988): 51.

The whole subject of the foibles of relationships between the sexes prompts me to recommend an amazing book (which has nothing to do with physiology, but instead focuses on how communication style typically differs between genders, often with disastrous results): Deborah Tannen's *You Just Don't Understand* (New York: Morrow, 1990), which should be required reading for all newlyweds.

The Pleasure (and Pain) of "Maybe"

Then there was the summer that Jonathan spent unsuccessfully mooning after Rebecca. Both were savanna baboons living in the Serengeti in East Africa, part of a troop that I have been studying intermittently for twenty-five years. Jonathan was an inoffensive beast, a gangly juvenile who had recently joined the troop, while Rebecca was the confident young daughter of one of the highest-ranking matriarchs. Jonathan had taken one look at Rebecca and developed a god-awful male baboon crush.

This took the form of Jonathan loping around after Rebecca. What he was probably after was for her to socially groom him, or maybe even something more intimate. What he was settling for, however, was the chance to socially groom her. And Rebecca was having none of that, wouldn't acknowledge his existence. She'd sit down to rest in the shade, to dig for some tuber in the ground, to hang out with her friends, and there'd be Jonathan, trying to groom her, and getting the cold, fur-covered shoulder.

By all logic, such spectacular lack of success should have caused Jonathan to give up, for the behavior to extinguish, to invoke some psychology jargon. But then, every so often, perhaps once a week, Rebecca would succumb to his devotion and let him groom her. Once, she even groomed him back for a few distracted seconds, leaving him in a baboonishly ecstatic state. And that was all it took. Aglow with these crumbs of attention, poor Jonathan would redouble his efforts over the next few days.

The whole soap opera frustrated me enormously. I was alone out in the middle of nowhere, probably badly in need of some social grooming myself; I was clearly having some transference issues with Jonathan. I sublimated this all into grand orations in my head: "Here are the nonhuman primate roots of our magnificent human capacity for gratification postponement. Here in this pathetic dork of a baboon and his willingness to keep trying again and again amid a pitiful success rate is the key to our greatness. Here is the fifty-year courtship of someone, the obsessive who spends a decade constructing a life-size replica of Elvis out of bottle caps, here's all of us forgoing immediate pleasure to get good grades to get into a good college to get a good job in order to get into the nursing home of our choice."

Soliloquies aside, some important issues were floating around there. What is it that gives us the power to do the harder thing, to be disciplined and opt for delayed gratification? And then there's the flip side of this question—why is the rare, intermittent reward, that hint that you might hit the lottery, so reinforcing? Why is gambling so addictive? Two recent studies go a long way toward explaining this, I believe.

We start with the frontal cortex, a brain region introduced at length in essay seven, "Why Are Dreams Dreamlike?" It's huge in us primates, taking up a proportionately larger percentage of our brains than in other species. The frontal cortex is involved in executive control, delayed gratification, long-term planning. It does this by sending inhibitory projections into the limbic system, a deeper, more ancient brain system involved in emotion and impulsivity. Furthermore, the frontal cortex excels at resisting stimulating inputs from the limbic system, ignoring tempting limbic whisperings like "Screw the studying for the exam, run amok instead." As noted in essay seven, people with tight, regimented, "repressive" personalities have elevated metabolic rates in the frontal cortex, while sociopaths have lower than normal ones. And if the frontal cortex is destroyed in a person, you have a "frontal" patient—sexually disinhibited, hyperaggressive, socially inappropriate. The frontal cortex is the closest thing we have to a neural basis for the superego.

So the frontal cortex is involved. But we've now merely redefined the problem, generating a more informed version of the same question. What is it that gives the frontal cortex the energy, the backbone, to ignore the siren call of the limbic system and to have the discipline to do the harder thing, to stick at something that is rarely rewarding? There has long been evidence that a major role is played by a projection into the frontal cortex (neuroanatomy phobics beware: from a brain region called the ventral tegmentum—but the name isn't important), one that releases the neurotransmitter dopamine. As a neurotransmitter closely associated with pleasure, dopamine is central to this story. Drugs like cocaine increase the dopamine signaling in this pathway. Animals will work like maniacs, pressing levers, forgoing every type of earthly pleasure, to get electrically stimulated in this dopaminergic "pleasure" pathway.

Thus, when is dopamine released in this pathway? Initially, there seemed to be an obvious answer: in response to reward. That's precisely how things seemed to work. Take a monkey (in whom you've implanted electrodes that allow you to monitor when this dopamine pathway becomes activated), give it some great reward from out of nowhere, and there'd be a burst of activity. Dopamine bathing the frontal cortex in the pleasure of reward.

But then a neuroscientist named Wolfram Schultz, then at the University of Fribourg in Switzerland, did some critical studies. He would train a monkey in a task. A light comes on, signaling the beginning of the reward period. This means that if the monkey presses a lever X number of times, after a few seconds' delay it will receive a bit of some desirable food. Thus one would predict that the dopaminergic pathway becomes activated after that food reward. But no.

When does activity peak? Right after the light comes on, before the monkey performs its task. In this context, the pleasurable dopamine isn't about reward. It's about the *anticipation* of reward. It's about mastery and expectation and confidence. It's "I know what that light means. I know the rules: *if* I press the lever, *then* I'm going to get some food. I'm all over this. This is going to be great." The pleasure is in the anticipation of a reward; from the standpoint of dopamine, the reward is an afterthought.

Psychologists refer to the period of anticipation, of expectation, of working for reward, as the "appetitive" stage, one filled with appetite, and call the stage that commences with reward the "consummatory" stage. What Schultz's findings show is that if you know your appetites are going to be sated, pleasure is more about the appetite than about the sating. The phenomenon reminded me of the terribly cynical observation of a classmate in college, one with a long string of tumultuously disastrous relationships: "A relationship is the price you pay for the anticipation of it."

So we've just sorted out the neurochemistry of putting up with thirty-year mortgages. There's the burst of dopaminergic pleasure once that light comes on, and all that is required is to train for longer and longer intervals between light and reward for those anticipatory bursts of dopamine to fuel increasing amounts of lever pressing. One of the recent papers fills in a critical piece in this story. Writing in the pages of *Nature,* Paul Phillips and colleagues from the University of North Carolina used some immensely fancy techniques to measure millisecond bursts of dopamine in the brains of rats and showed with the best time resolution to date that the burst comes just before the behavior. Then, in the clincher, they artificially stimulated dopamine release (rather than having it triggered by the light cue), and suddenly the rat starts lever pressing. The dopamine fuels the behavior.

All of this seems to explain a scenario that could have been played out on the savanna, if there were a tightly coupled If/Then clause going on with Jonathan and Rebecca. Jonathan sits dozing in the equatorial sun. If Rebecca appears, dramatic entrance at the other end of the field, windswept fur, the whole deal . . . an appetitive light goes on in Jonathan's brain, his ventral tegmentum gets all hyperactive, releasing dopamine like mad, providing his frontal cortex the discipline to walk him across the field toward her, Wagner in the background, with the anticipatory certainty that she is going to let him groom her.

But there was no If/Then occurring. There was an If/Maybe. Jonathan pursues Rebecca, and it only works some of the time. And that reinforces him like crazy. Why does coyness work? Why is intermittent reinforcement so much more enticing than a sure thing? Why is gambling so addictive? In a second paper, published in *Science*, Christopher Fiorillo and colleagues (including Schultz) revealed this with a brilliant experiment.

Back to the scenario before. Light comes on, press lever, get reward. Now formalize the Rebecca scenario, introduce the Maybe. Light comes on, press lever, get the reward a few seconds later . . . but only an average of 50 percent of the time. Right on that fulcrum of uncertainty, maybe yes, maybe no. And remarkably, the total amount of activity of that dopamine pathway increases. And even more remarkable is the way that it does. Light comes on in the fifty-fifty scenario and there's the usual dopamine rise, fueling the lever pressing. And, lever pressing completed, a *second* phase of dopamine release begins, gradually increasing, peaking right around the time that the reward would happen if it is going to occur. Suppose the experimenters decreased the degree of uncertainty, of unpredictability; light comes on, lever is pressed, but now there's a 25 percent or a 75 percent chance of reward. Note how different 25 percent and 75 percent are, in that they represent opposite trends toward the chances of reward. But what they have in common is that they carry less of a maybe than the 50 percent scenario. And now that secondary rise in dopaminergic activity occurs, but to a lesser extent. The total amount of dopamine released is highest under conditions of greatest uncertainty as to whether a reward will occur.

And this explains why intermittent reinforcements can be so profoundly reinforcing. And why the chance of a huge reward, even the most ludicrously remote Maybe of a chance, can be so addictive, spiraling wild-eyed gamblers into squandering the kids' food money in the casino.

These findings dovetail nicely with a literature in stress physiology showing the dark side of Maybe. We've just seen that a reward that has a decent chance of occurring can be more reinforcing than the utterly predictable one. And conversely, a punishment that has a decent chance of occurring can be vastly more stressful than a predictable one. For the same punishment out there in the real world, unpredictable versions carry the greater risk of stress hormone levels and blood pressure rising, and of stress-related disease occurring. As a naturalistic example, the primatologist Joan Silk of UCLA presents evidence that one of the skills honed by alpha male baboons to keep the competition off-kilter is to be brutally aggressive at times in utterly random, unpredictable ways. The corrosive core of terrorism is the orange-alert world of never knowing where or when.

We big-cortex primates work hard to make sense of the cause and effect in the world around us. Making sense of causal links that are probabilistic—A leads to B only some of the time—is not trivial. A frequent myth in both cognitive science and economics is that we go about trying to understand causality in a logical way. But instead, that gleaming, sensible cortex sits there marinating in all sorts of frothy, hormonal, affective influences, and that can make for rational assessments being pretty irrational. And thus we wind up finding the chance of punishment to be more stressful than the certainty of punishment. And on the flip side, if the lottery payoff is big enough, we decide that we've got *the* lucky number, no matter what the odds, and we're soon going to be in social grooming heaven.

And Jonathan and Rebecca? Well, she remained more interested in the high-ranking, prime-aged guys, and he eventually got over it. Except for one wild twenty-four-hour consortship they had a few years later, on a day that she was at the peak of her ovulatory cycle. But that's another story.

⚘ NOTES AND FURTHER READING ⚘

The two papers mentioned are Phillips P, Stuber G, Heien M, Wightman R, and Carelli R, "Subsecond dopamine release promotes cocaine seeking," *Nature* 422 (2003): 614; and Fiorillo C, Tobler P, and Schultz W, "Discrete coding of reward probability and uncertainty by dopamine neurons," *Science* 299 (2003): 1,898. For an overview of Schultz's enormous contributions to understanding the functioning of the frontal cortex, see Schultz W, Tremblay L, and Holerman J, "Reward processing in primate orbitofrontal cortex and basal ganglia," *Cerebral Cortex* 10 (2000): 272. A recent, immensely clever paper shows that the frontal cortex not only plays a role in modifying behavior as a function of anticipation, but also as a function of regret: Camille N, Coricelli G, Sallet J, Pradat-Diehl P, Duhamel J, and Sirigu A, "The involvement of the orbitofrontal cortex in the experience of regret," *Science* 304 (2004): 1,167.

As one thinks about the role of the frontal cortex in regulating and restraining our behaviors in anticipation and gratification postponement, one must immediately ask, What happens when the frontal cortex is damaged? With increasing frequency, this winds up being an arena in which science can be at odds with the legal system. For a discussion of this, see Sapolsky R, "The frontal cortex and the criminal justice system," Transactions of the Royal Philosophical Society, *Biological Sciences* (2004): 359, 1,787.

Finally, for more scurrilous gossip about Jonathan and Rebecca, see Sapolsky R, *A Primate's Memoir* (New York: Scribner, 2002).

Stress and Your Shrinking Brain

Every now and then, someone with a medical problem needs a CT scan or MRI of the brain. With any luck, some horrible disease is ruled out, everything is okay, and offhandedly, the doctor shows the patient the scan. If it's her first one, the patient will probably get the willies. Unlike pictures of other organs, which inspire a bemused, "Hey, lookie here, that's my liver," brain scans provoke awe. That's your brain in there, with its convoluted surface and all those mysterious subsections. Rookie med students feel the same disquiet in anatomy class when they first hold a cadaver's brain in their hands. The same uneasiness makes neurosurgeons joke, "There go the piano lessons," when they cut into gray matter. The brain, after all, is the Seat of the Soul, the Big Enchilada of Consciousness, the organ of Me-ness. From this mass of tissue that vaguely resembles marinated tofu emanates a person.

So most of us feel a rather proprietary concern about the state of our brains. And thus, it becomes mighty interesting when something pops up that may be dramatically decreasing the size of a part of an adult's brain. Check out the brain of a chronic alcoholic and one region may be badly disintegrated; autopsy someone who was exposed to lots of organic toxins and you'll see damage in another brain area. And as the point of this piece, there's another brain region that may atrophy in response to certain types of serious stress.

Take some green eighteen-year-old, stick him in a uniform and ship him off to a war, and now expose him to something truly horrific, even by the standards of human violence—say, a battle in which he is one of the sole survivors of his unit, where he has watched his closest buddies slaughtered. Some rare, inexplicable supermen come out of the experience completely unfazed or, inconceivably, even strengthened by it, having found life's meaning during that moment when the world melted around them, when the very air seemed on fire. Your average guy, however, definitely comes out a lot worse for the wear. He may suffer from nightmares afterward, guilt at having survived, an estrangement from loved ones back home who can never understand what he went through. And that's if he's lucky. But then one subset is seemingly damaged forever.

In the First World War, it was called shell shock, producing men who, as octogenarians, would still shake and reflexively leap for cover when a door slammed. Something similar was called battle fatigue by World War II. And in the modern psychiatric parlance, the long-lasting residues are called PTSD, for post-traumatic stress disorder. It's not just restricted to combat trauma. Surviving the carnage of yet another choirboy-next-door-goes-postal-with-an- automatic-weapon, a gang rape, a childhood of sexual abuse, surviving Auschwitz, or, as studies suggest will be relevant to tens to hundreds of thousands of people, experiencing 9/11 firsthand in New York— all are settings that produce the broken person who gets that acronym.

According to the American Psychiatric Association, patients with PTSD suffer for months to years from flashbacks, nightmares and other sleep problems, emotional numbness or outbursts, loss of pleasure, an inappropriate startle reflex, and problems with memory and concentration. Those last two symptoms have prompted recent brain-imaging studies.

Memory problems might arise from subtle microscopic conditions: something wrong in the way a few critical neurons produce or use a particular neurotransmitter, or trouble with the enzymes that degrade a neurotransmitter, or with the receptor for it or the intracellular messengers it triggers. In the last few years, however, some neuroscientists have begun to look at the bigger picture, generating magnetic resonance images of PTSD patients' brains and carefully measuring the volumes of the organs' many bewildering regions. The researchers have dotted their *i*'s and crossed their *t*'s like good scientists, controlling for the depression and substance abuse that often accompany PTSD and controlling for total brain size, age, sex, and education. And recently, groups working independently at Yale, Harvard, Emory University, and the University of California at San Diego have all reported the same thing: in individuals suffering from PTSD due to chronic trauma, an important area of the brain called the hippocampus tends to be smaller than average. This has been reported for PTSD associated with combat trauma or childhood abuse—repeated, chronic traumas—and seems not to occur when PTSD arises from a single trauma, such as a car accident.

To the cognoscenti, that was big news. There're regions of the brain that have been swallowing up earnest grad students like quicksand for decades without yielding a clue as to their function. But the hippocampus is well-explored terrain. It's critical to forming long-term memories and retrieving old ones, to the management of explicit, conscious memory. When pairs of hippocampal neurons are repeatedly stimulated, their connections become stronger: shazam, those neurons have learned something. Surgically destroy the hippocampus, as has been done in a zillion lab rats and in one famous neurological patient only known as HM, and there is complete destruction of some major types of memory. Have the hippocampus ravaged by Alzheimer's disease and you've got similar problems.

So the hippocampus is smaller than normal in these PTSD individuals. In most of the studies, it is only the hippocampus that is shrunken; the rest of the brain is fine. And the atrophy is not trivial. For example, Tamara Gurvits, Roger Pitman, and colleagues at Harvard have reported a greater than 25 percent average atrophy in one side of the hippocampus in their combat PTSD patients. *Twenty-five percent*—that's like reporting that an emotional trauma eliminates one of the four chambers of the heart. This is likely to be a hippocampus seriously out of whack, and findings of Douglas Bremner and colleagues at Emory support that notion—typically, when a person is given a memory task, the metabolic rate of the hippocampus increases, reflecting the energy costs of that brain region having to kick into gear. In contrast, the same memory task fails to stimulate hippocampal metabolism in people with PTSD, fitting well with the picture of memory deficits typically seen in such people.

So that's the scientific observation that a lot of people are agreeing on all of a sudden. The debate, of course, is *why* a small hippocampus and PTSD go together. One possible explanation has been on the scene for a couple of decades and has been reframed for the PTSD story by Bremner. Its basic premise is that the stress of the trauma, and/or of the post-traumatic period, causes the hippocampus to shrink. And there's a lot of reason to think that this is going on. During stress, whether of a physical or a psychological nature, your adrenal gland secretes loads of a class of steroid hormones called glucocorticoids (which were briefly introduced in essay two, "A Gene for Nothing"). Most people are familiar with the human version of glucocorticoids, namely hydrocortisone, or with synthetic versions, such as prednisone or dexamethasone.

To begin to see what stress might have to do with a shrunken hippocampus, we have to get a sense of what these hormones do. Glucocorticoids are essential in your bloodstream for surviving a stressful sprint across the savanna with a hungry leopard on your tail, as they help mobilize energy to those exercising thigh muscles and shut down unessentials (such as growth or reproduction), which can wait for more auspicious times. And when secreted only transiently in response to an acute stressor, glucocorticoids enhance memory, increasing the strength of those excitatory connections between neurons in the hippocampus. This is the realm of remembering where we were when hearing news of some disaster, or when we can recall the details and nuances of that brief encounter with the mugger as if it occurred yesterday and lasted hours.

For 99 percent of the beasts on this planet, stress is about three minutes of screaming terror as you sprint for your life on the savanna, after which it's either over with or you're over with. Problems begin because we cognitively sophisticated humans are capable of secreting glucocorticoids chronically for reasons of sustained psychological and social stress. And in contrast to the helpful actions of glucocorticoids in the face of an acute, physical stressor, too much of the hormones in response to chronic stress, and all sorts of stress-related problems such as high blood pressure, reproductive impairments, and immune suppression, become more likely.

Because the hippocampus has lots of receptors for glucocorticoids, it's one of the parts of the brain most sensitive to these hormones. And it turns out that glucocorticoids can damage neurons in the hippocampus of rodents and primates. Work from my laboratory and others has shown that this happens through a number of routes. For starters, a few days of elevated glucocorticoid levels can "endanger" a hippocampal neuron, making it harder for it to survive a neurological crisis such as a seizure, or a period of no oxygen or glucose, as occurs during cardiac arrest. Next, over a few weeks to months, glucocorticoids will cause the branchlike connections between hippocampal neurons to shrivel; once the stress or the glucocorticoid exposure ends, the branches slowly grow back. Finally, when glucocorticoid levels stay high enough for long enough— months or years—they can destroy hippocampal neurons.

These findings have unnerved some clinicians, given that patients with a variety of diseases are often administered high-dose glucocorticoids for a long time (and studies suggest that those high doses do impair memory), and because the body itself secretes a ton of these hormones during neurological crises. Can excessive glucocorticoids damage the human hippocampus? Seemingly.

Consider Cushing's disease, where any of a number of types of tumors produces astronomically high glucocorticoid levels. Monica Starkman and colleagues at the University of Michigan have found atrophied hippocampi on MRI scans in people with this disease. The rest of the brain is fine, and the higher the levels of glucocorticoids in the bloodstream of these people, the smaller the hippocampus and the more memory problems the patient experiences. When the tumor is corrected and glucocorticoid levels go back to normal, the hippocampus slowly returns to the normal size, suggesting that those branches may be shriveling away and then growing back.

So in the Bremner model, stress-induced glucocorticoid secretion in PTSD shrinks the hippocampus. An alternative model comes from Rachel Yehuda and colleagues at Mt. Sinai School of Medicine in New York. Surprisingly, in about half the studies that have examined this question, people with PTSD have lower than normal levels of glucocorticoids, rather than elevated levels (something first reported by Yehuda). Her group's careful work has shown that such cases of low glucocorticoid levels are due to the brain being more sensitive to the regulatory effects of glucocorticoids, resulting in less secretion (somewhat akin to making a thermostat more sensitive to minor changes in temperature). Thus, in their view, the problem is not too much of these stress hormones during the trauma and/or the post-traumatic period. The problem, instead, is that there's too much *sensitivity* to these hormones during the post-traumatic period. In either case, interestingly, there is a likely culprit, a stress-related hormone known to do bad things to the hippocampus and memory under other circumstances.

Insofar as glucocorticoids are involved, what might they be doing to the hippocampus? As noted, they can cause the interconnections between neurons to shrivel, and with the abatement of stress, those interconnections regrow, which probably explains the normalizing of hippocampal volume in Cushing's disease. But in PTSD, the atrophy can persist for years or decades after the trauma, arguing against the "shriveled cables" model. So maybe the loss of hippocampal volume is due to the glucocorticoids actually killing the neurons. Meanwhile, another possibility arises. If you'd taken introductory neuroscience anytime in the last thousand years, you'd have been taught one of the dogmas of the field, namely that the adult brain does not make new neurons. In recent years, it has become clear that that is wrong—new neurons are being made all the time, replacing ones being lost, with most of the "neurogenesis" occurring in the hippocampus. And, as a really provocative finding, stress and glucocorticoids are about the strongest inhibitors of adult neurogenesis out there. Thus, another possibility is that the hippocampal atrophy in PTSD is due to inhibition of neurogenesis, with glucocorticoids blocking the birth of neurons that should otherwise have been taking their place in hippocampal circuits.

All of this is conjecture at this point and will remain that way until someone studies the brains of PTSD individuals after they've died, taking on the immensely obsessive task of counting the number of neurons in the hippocampi of these brains (versus appropriately matched control brains), measuring the length and complexity of neuronal cables within the hippocampus, and so on. This will not be a job for the fainthearted, but it is critical.

Amid this theorizing, there's the possibility that neither trauma nor the posttraumatic period atrophy the hippocampus. Perhaps the causality is switched around. Put a bunch of soldiers through some unspeakable hell of combat, and it's typically only a subset of them, perhaps 15 to 20 percent, who get the PTSD. The size of the hippocampus varies from one person to the next, and maybe it's only people who go into a trauma with a small hippocampus who are vulnerable to PTSD. Maybe that person processes information differently, forms memories in a different way, is more at risk for flashbacks. Pitman and colleagues presented some indirect support for this possibility, reporting that soldiers who wind up with PTSD have disproportionately high rates of "soft" neurological signs—not out-and-out neurological diseases but some minor red flags, such as delayed development landmarks, higher than average rates of learning disorders, and low IQ.

More recently, Pitman's group has followed up with a really interesting finding. Sleuthing through the Veterans Administration records, they found a gold mine of a database—a small number of sets of identical twins where one was sent off to Vietnam and the other stayed home. First examining the twins who went to Vietnam and experienced combat trauma, they identified the subset that had gotten PTSD. Brain imaging showed the usual finding—smaller than expected hippocampi compared with those who experienced combat trauma but didn't get PTSD. And then they looked at the twins who stayed back home. Remarkably, the twins of the small-hippocampi PTSDers had equally small hippocampi. This strongly supports the idea that a small hippocampus came before Vietnam in these men, and that it increased their vulnerability to combat PTSD.

This is a striking study. I see two problems, though. There's been at least one study showing that the worse the combat trauma experienced by soldiers, the worse the hippocampal volume loss later on (a finding reported earlier by Pitman's group). This sure fits a model where trauma gives rise to a shrinking hippocampus, rather than a small hippocampus giving rise to vulnerability to PTSD. As a second issue, in some types of trauma the majority of victims succumb to PTSD—multiple-rape survivors, for example, have about a 90 percent PTSD rate. And in that scenario, you can't argue that a smaller than average hippocampus places you in the minority likely to succumb to PTSD, since the vast majority succumbs.

Thus, it's not clear if the small hippocampus is due to dead neurons, shriveled neurons, or new neurons that failed to be born, and critical studies require postmortem counting of neurons in the brain. And it's not clear whether the small hippocampus precedes and biases toward PTSD or is a consequence of trauma and PTSD. In this case, the critical study requires getting brain images of people *before* they experience trauma, then following up with more brain imaging after they do or don't succumb to PTSD. While this may be apocryphal, a year ago, as U.S. forces were poised to invade Iraq, a rumor swept through the community of brain-imaging neuroscientists that the military was doing baseline brain imaging on Special Forces soldiers heading off to the front.

So we've got scientists disagreeing, experiments to be done, grants to be written. What does this all mean? Let's start with what this *doesn't* mean. At present, there isn't a shred of evidence to link everyday stress—traffic jams, money worries, crummy bosses, unhappy relationships—to neurons keeling over dead or a hippocampus shrinking. Those stressors are not so hot for things like blood pressure and may result in hippocampal neurons not functioning at their best (explaining why the stressor of, say, pulling an all-nighter just before a final doesn't do great things for memory the next day). But the neurons almost certainly remain intact.

As another caveat, the phenomenon of the branches in neurons in the hippocampus shriveling up from stress and later recovering has provided an irresistible metaphor for some folks seeking an explanation for "recovered memory." That is the business about the memory of some horrendous trauma being utterly repressed, only to then be recovered years or decades later. Lives have been destroyed over this incendiary issue—either the victim of the trauma (in one interpretation of events), left to wait decades for justice because of the workings of memory, or the victim of the false accusation (in the counterview), consumed in this season's Salem witch hunt. Civil war has nearly broken out among the neuropsychologists over this one, so let me tread lightly here—I will simply say that I have seen no scientific evidence for how such recovered memories might work, no supposed cases of them documented to be legitimate in a way that should satisfy a rigorous scientist, and plenty of scientific explanations for why various claims have not been legitimate.

And what do these findings mean? It if turns out that a small hippocampus is a risk factor for PTSD, neuroanatomy should be taken into account as readily as the presence of a heart murmur when considering who's going to get shipped off to battle. And if the atrophy is a consequence of the trauma or the post-trauma period, the scientists then have their usual marching orders—go and figure out how this works so that we can learn how to prevent it.

But these findings should mean something larger as well. For most of us, all the alarming lectures in the world about how we are endangering our environment don't have the power of that first, iconic picture from the moon of Earth—tiny, vastly alone, fragile. And for most of us, reading about the Nazis can't take our breath away like a visit to the Holocaust Museum, with its room filled beyond number with the shoes of the murdered. We need concrete images when trying to grasp the ungraspable. And thus a thousand people writing a thousand words of testimonial each about the consequences of human violence may not have the impact of one picture, even one as literally and figuratively cerebral as that of a brain scan. Look what they did to my brain. Look what they did to me.

✧ NOTES AND FURTHER READING ✧

PTSD: all standard psychiatry textbooks have good descriptions of PTSD, and Web sites for both the American Psychiatric Association and the National Institute of Mental Health have good, accessible information on the disorder.

PTSD in the aftermath of 9/11: A number of studies have been carried out using approaches that can predict, with a decent degree of accuracy, who is going to succumb to PTSD in the New York metropolitan area following 9/11. Alarmingly, the studies, using some very different approaches, have come up with similar estimates—hundreds of thousands of cases emerging in the coming years. These reports can be found in Schlenger W, Caddell J, Ebert L, Jordan B, Rourke K, Wilson D, Thalji L, Dennis J, Fairbank J, and Kulka R, "Psychological reactions to terrorist attacks: findings from the National Study of

Americans' Reactions to September 11," *Journal of the American Medical Association* 288 (2002): 581; and Galea S, Resnick H, Ahern J, Gold J, Bucuvalas M, Kilpatrick D, Stuber J, and Vlahov D, "PTSD in Manhattan, New York City, after the September 11th terrorist attacks," *Journal of Urban Health: Bulletin of the New York Academy of Medicine* 79 (2002): 340.

For some of the reports of small hippocampal volumes in PTSD, see Bremner J, Randall P, Scott T, Bronen R, et al., "MRI-based measurement of hippocampal volume in patients with combat-related PTSD," *American Journal of Psychiatry* 152 (1995): 973; Gurvits T, Shenton M, Hokama H, Ohta H, Lasko N, Gilbertson M, et al., "Magnetic resonance imaging study of hippocampal volume in chronic, combat-related post-traumatic stress disorder," *Biological Psychiatry* 40 (1996): 1,091; and Bremner J, Randall P, Vermetten E, Staib L, Bronen A, et al., "Magnetic resonance imaging–based measurement of hippocampal volume in PTSD related to childhood physical and sexual abuse—a preliminary report," *Biological Psychiatry* 41 (1997): 23. This whole subject is reviewed at length in Sapolsky R, "Glucocorticoids and hippocampal atrophy in neuropsychiatric disorders," *Archives of General Psychiatry* 57 (2000): 925.

For a masterful review of the neurobiology of memory (and what the hippocampus has to do with it), see Squire L, *Memory and Brain* (New York: Oxford University Press, 1987). For another excellent (and more current) overview, see Eichenbaum H, "The hippocampus and declarative memory: cognitive mechanisms and neural codes," *Behavioral Brain Research* 127 (2001): 199.

The dichotomy between the stress-response being adaptive when it is mobilized transiently for an acute physical stressor, and increasing the risk of disease when it is mobilized chronically for reasons of psychological stress, is the central concept of Sapolsky R, *Why Zebras Don't Get Ulcers: A Guide to Stress, Stress-Related Diseases, and Coping,* 3rd ed. (New York: Henry Holt, 2004). The effects of stress on memory are reviewed at length in Sapolsky R, "Stress and cognition," in Gazzaniga M, ed., *The Cognitive Neurosciences,* 3rd ed. (Cambridge, MA: MIT Press, 2004): 1,031.

The argument for how the hippocampus is likely to be shrinking in response to trauma and PTSD is summarized in Sapolsky R, "Why stress is bad for your brain," *Science* 273 (1996): 749; and Bremner J, *Is Stress Bad for Your Brain?* (New York: Norton, 2002). As an example of findings of suppressed, rather than elevated, glucocorticoid levels in PTSD, see Yehuda R, Southwick S, Nussbaum E, Giller E, and Mason J, "Low urinary cortisol in PTSD," *Journal of Nervous and Mental Diseases* 178 (1991): 366.

For a good review of the revolution concerning neurogenesis in the adult brain, see Gould E and Gross C, "Neurogenesis in adult mammals: some progress and problems," *Journal of Neuroscience* 22 (2002): 619.

The report concerning small hippocampi in identical twins is found in Gilbertson M, Shenton M, Ciszewski A, Kasai K, Lasko N, Orr S, and Pitman R, "Smaller hippocampal volume predicts pathologic vulnerability to psychological trauma," *Nature Neuroscience* 5 (2002): 1,242. An accompanying commentary in the same issue is Sapolsky R, "Chicken, eggs and hippocampal atrophy," page 1,111.

As a final disclaimer, it should be noted that this subject is one of the fastest-changing of any of the topics covered in this book, and thus this piece may be obsolete a week after it goes to the printer.

Bugs in the Brain

L ike most scientists, I attend professional meetings every now and then, and I recently returned from the annual meeting of something called the Society for Neuroscience, an organization of most of Earth's brain researchers. Now, this is one of the more intellectually assaultive experiences that you can imagine. For one thing, there's about twenty-eight thousand of us science nerds jammed into one convention center, and this begins to feel pretty nutty after a while— for an entire week, go into any restaurant, elevator, bathroom, and the folks standing next to you will be having some animated discussion about squid axons. Then there's finding out about the science itself. The meeting has fourteen thousand lectures and posters, a completely overwhelming amount of information. And of the subset of those posters that are essential for you to check, a bunch you never get to see because of the enthusiastic crowds in front of them, another turns out to be in some language you don't even recognize, and then there's the critical poster that reports every experiment you planned to do for the next five years. And amid this all, there's this shared realization that despite the zillions of us slaving away at the subject, we still know squat about how the brain works.

My own low point came one afternoon as I sat on the steps of the convention center, bludgeoned by all this information and a general sense of ignorance. My eyes focused on a stagnant, murky puddle of water by the curb, and I realized that some microscopic bug festering in that puddle probably knew more about the brain than all of us neuroscientists combined.

My demoralized insight was prompted by a recent, extraordinary paper about how certain parasites control the brain of their host. Most of us know that bacteria, protozoans, and viruses have astonishingly sophisticated ways of using animal bodies for their own purposes. They hijack our cells, our energy, and our lifestyles so they can thrive. As one example of their cleverness, some viruses go latent in the bodies of mammals and just wait there, biding their time. When does it make sense for them to come out of latency, to activate and replicate? When the mammal's immune system is suppressed, not at its best. When are immune systems suppressed? During stress. Contained in the DNA of these viruses are detectors that are activated by stress hormones. So get good and stressed by a chronic illness, starvation, a string of final exams, and these viruses know it, come roaring out of latency to replicate while your immune system is at its worst. And suddenly you get that herpes cold-sore flare-up. Then there are tropical protozoans like trypanosomes that invade your body and defeat you because every few weeks they're able to switch the identifying fingerprint of proteins on their cell surfaces, just as your immune system was about to recognize and attack them. Or then there are blood flukes like schistosomes, which don't even bother switching identities. Instead, they steal yours—cloaking themselves in your own identifying cell-surface proteins, so that they are immunologically invisible.

But in many ways, the most dazzling and fiendish thing that such parasites have evolved—and the subject that occupied my musings that day—is their ability to change a host's behavior for their own ends. Some textbook examples involve ectoparasites, organisms that colonize the surface of the body. For instance, certain mites of the genus *Antennophorus* ride on the backs of ants and, by stroking an ant's mouthparts, can trigger a reflex that culminates in the ant's disgorging food for the mite to feed on. A species of pinworm of the genus *Syphacia* lays eggs on a rodent's skin, the eggs secrete a substance that causes itchiness, the rodent grooms the itchy spot with its teeth, the eggs get ingested, and once inside the rodent they happily hatch.

Bizarre as these examples are, things get even stranger when considering the ways that parasites manipulate our behavior from *inside* us. Some examples involve parasites with sequential hosts—they go through one life stage inside the body of some intermediate host, then reproduce or replicate inside the body of a definitive host. The challenge is to move from the former to the latter host. So the parasite may damage the muscles of an intermediate host, blind it, parasitize the host's food, forcing it to concentrate on foraging instead of looking over its shoulder—all ways to increase the likelihood of the intermediate host, along with the parasite inside, winding up in the predator who is the definitive host.

Things get even weirder when considering parasites that alter the function of the nervous system itself. Sometimes, this is done indirectly, by manipulating hormones that affect the nervous system. There are barnacles *(Sacculina granifera),* a form of crustacean, that attach to male sand crabs and secrete a feminizing hormone that induces maternal behavior. The zombified crabs then migrate out to sea with brooding females and make depressions in the sand ideal for dispersing larvae. The males, naturally, won't be releasing any. But the barnacles will. And if the barnacle infects a female, it induces the same maternal behavior—after atrophying the female's ovaries, a practice called parasitic castration.

The ultimate, though, is when a parasite gets into the brain itself. These are microscopic, mostly viruses, rather than relatively gargantuan creatures like mites, pinworms, and barnacles. Once one of these tiny parasites is inside the brain, it remains fairly sheltered from immune attack, and it can go to work diverting neural machinery to its own advantage.

The rabies virus is one such parasite. There are lots of ways rabies could have evolved to move between hosts. The virus didn't have to go anywhere near the brain itself. It could have developed a trick similar to the one employed by the agents that cause nose colds—namely, to irritate the nerve endings in your nasal passages, causing you to sneeze and spritz viral replicates all over the person sitting in front of you at the movies. Or the virus could have evolved an ability to induce an insatiable desire to lick someone, thereby passing on virus shed into the saliva. Instead, as we all know, rabies can cause its host to become aggressive so the virus can jump into another host via saliva that gets into the wounds.

Just think about this. Scads of neurobiologists study the neural basis of aggression—the pathways in the brain that are involved, the relevant neurotransmitters, the interactions between genes and environment, modulation by hormones, and so on. There are conferences on the subject, doctoral theses, petty academic squabbles, nasty tenure disputes, the works—while all along the rabies virus "knows" just which neurons to infect to make someone rabid.

Despite how impressive these viral effects are, there's still room for improvement. This is because of the parasite's nonspecificity. If you're a rabid animal, you might bite one of the few creatures that rabies does not replicate well in, such as a rabbit. So while the behavioral effects of infection of the brain with parasites can be pretty dazzling, if the effects are too broad, that parasite could wind up in a dead-end host.

Which brings us to a beautifully specific case of brain control and the paper I mentioned earlier, by Manuel Berdoy and colleagues at Oxford University. Berdoy and associates study a parasite called *Toxoplasma gondii*. In a toxoplasmic utopia, life consists of a two-host sequence of rodent and cat. The protozoan gets ingested by a rodent, where it forms cysts throughout the body, particularly the brain. The rodent gets eaten by a cat, where *Toxoplasma* reproduces. The cat sheds the parasite in the feces, which, in one of those circles of life, is nibbled at by rodents. The whole scenario hinges on specificity, in that cats are the only species in which *Toxoplasma* can reproduce and be shed. Thus, *Toxoplasma* wouldn't want its carrier rodent to get picked off by a hawk, or its cat feces to get ingested by a dung beetle. Mind you, the parasite can infect all sorts of other species; it simply has to wind up in a cat if it wants to reproduce.

This potential to infect other species is the reason why all those "what to do during pregnancy" books advise banning the cat and its litter box from the house and warn pregnant women against gardening if cats are wandering about. If toxoplasma from cat feces gets into a pregnant woman, it can get into the fetus, potentially causing neurological damage.

Thus, well-informed pregnant women get skittish of cats. And the extraordinary trick that *Toxoplasma* has evolved is to make rodents *un*skittish of cats. All good rodents avoid cats—a behavior ethologists call a fixed action pattern, in that the rodent doesn't develop the aversion due to trial and error (since there aren't likely to be many opportunities to learn from one's errors around cats). Instead, feline phobia is hardwired. And it is accomplished through olfaction, through pheromones, the chemical odorant signals that animals release. Rodents instinctually shy away from the smell of a cat—even rodents that have never seen a cat in their lives, who are the descendants of hundreds of generations of lab animals. Except for those rodents infected with *Toxoplasma*. As Berdoy and colleagues showed, rodents selectively lose their aversion to and fear of cat pheromones. Instead, they become attracted to the smell.

Now, this is not some generic case of a parasite messing with the head of the intermediate host and making it scatterbrained and vulnerable. Everything else seems pretty intact in the rodents. The social status of the animal doesn't change in its dominance hierarchy. It is still interested in mating and thus, de facto, in the pheromones of the opposite sex. It can still distinguish other odors (for example, of itself, or of a perfectly benign bunny). All that happens is that the rodent no longer recoils from cat pheromones and instead gravitates toward them. This is flabbergasting. This is like someone getting infected with a brain parasite that has no effect whatsoever on the person's thoughts, emotions, SAT scores, or television preferences, but, to complete its life cycle, generates an irresistible urge to go to the zoo, scale a fence, and French-kiss the pissiest-looking polar bear. A parasite-induced fatal attraction, as Berdoy's team noted in the title of its paper.

Obviously, more research is needed. I say this not only because that's obligatory around this point in any article about science, but because this finding is just so intrinsically cool that someone has to figure out how this works. And because—permit me a Stephen Jay Gould moment, if you will—it provides ever more evidence that evolution is amazing. Amazing in ways that are counterintuitive. There is a deeply entrenched idea that evolution is directional and progressive. If you believe this, your thinking goes something like this: invertebrates are more primitive than vertebrates, mammals are the most evolved of vertebrates, primates are the genetically fanciest mammals, and so on until, ultimately, there's seeming scientific proof for the evolutionary superiority of whatever race, ethnicity, or bowling league you belong to. And it is simply wrong.

So remember, creatures are out there that can control brains (and, in the process, can run circles around neuroscientists). My reflection on a curbside puddle brought me to the opposite conclusion from what Narcissus reached in his watery reflection. We need phylogenetic humility. We are certainly not the most evolved species around, nor the least vulnerable. Nor the cleverest.

⟶ NOTES AND FURTHER READING ⟵

For a good general overview of the subject, see Moore J, *Parasites and the Behavior of Animals* (Cambridge: Oxford University Press, 2002).

The amazing *Toxoplasma* study is reported in Berdoy M, Webster J, and Macdonald D, "Fatal attraction in rats infected with *Toxo-*

plasma gondii," *Proceedings of the Royal Society of London,* B 267 (2000): 1,591.

Mites riding on the backs of ants, pinworms, itchy rodents, and barnacle-infected crabs, are all discussed in Moore J, *Parasites and the Behavior of Animals.*

A lot of the essays in this book represent hit-and-run obsessions— for a couple of months, I get crazed about some topic, read endlessly on it, drive my wife to distraction with my monologues on the topic. I eventually write something, getting it out of my system, thereby freeing me to fixate on a next topic. This essay started this way as well. However, that astonishing report about the behavioral effects of *Toxoplasma* has continued to intrigue me sufficiently so that I recently recruited a superb young scientist, Dr. Ajai Vyas, to my lab to try to figure out what *Toxoplasma* is doing in the brain of a rodent. Stay tuned.

Nursery Crimes

Jennifer Bush seemed a heartbreaking example of bad medical luck. The child had had medical ills since infancy—tough, multi-system problems that tenaciously resisted treatment, crippling her digestive system and urinary tract. She seemed to have immune problems as well, for despite her normal white-blood-cell counts, she repeatedly festered with a variety of bacterial infections in her gut and bladder. By age nine, Jennifer had been hospitalized more than two hundred times and had undergone forty operations, including removal of her gallbladder, her appendix, part of her intestines. And still she did not improve. Her plight was a long-standing mystery—until it was solved, not by her doctors, but by the police.

To begin to understand what had happened to Jennifer Bush, one must confront a vexing question: What things are okay to do to a child? Whom does a child belong to? And should a child belong to anyone?

This issue was at the core of what caused a bunch of my friends to lose religion as adolescents. We would marvel at the injustices of the Exodus story. What about the horses? we would ask. Why should they have been drowned in the Red Sea? And what about the soldiers who got drowned? I bet a lot of them didn't have any choice in the matter.

But the episode most likely to shake one's faith was obvious: And what about the killing of the firstborn, the babies, how'd they get mixed up in this? Our Sunday-school teachers would dutifully fill us in on how the situation was more complicated than we appreciated. You see, Pharaoh was not just a man. This was a turf war between Yahweh, God of the Israelites, and Pharaoh, God of the Egyptians, with no holds barred. Egyptian cows, horses, crops, loyal servants, even babies, all belonged to Pharaoh and were thus fair game. The ten plagues became just rubouts against the family of this *global parentis* godfather.

This is not the sort of explanation that would still cut it with most folks, the idea of damaging a child to punish or test a parent—these days, if Abraham threatened to slit his son Isaac's throat because he and his god had some issues to work out, a likely result would be a visit from the child welfare authorities. Nevertheless, most people consider children to be partial extensions of adults, and rightly so. Children need their parents to make important decisions about their health care, their diet, and their education—otherwise they would spend entire childhoods eating doughnuts and watching TV. But how much oversight is appropriate? Is a child a mere extension of his or her parents, the school system, the tribe, the state?

These questions have generated some pretty extreme viewpoints, some of which resemble horror stories. At one end of the spectrum are those who argue that adults have no right to impose anything at all on children. An academic version of this is found in the work of Thomas Szasz, one of psychiatry's most persistent nudniks, who spent a career questioning and poking at all sorts of cherished beliefs. He proclaimed mental illness a "myth," a labeling system for the powerful to shunt away troublesome thinkers. He argued that psychiatry could only be carried out with consenting individuals, calling involuntary psychiatric treatment rape of the patient, and that no child could be the consenting equal of an adult psychiatrist, making child psychiatry illegitimate.

As another example, a few years back, a loony reductio of the child-as-free-agent idea was promulgated by the mother of Jessica Dubroff. She was the seven-year-old whose gimmick of becoming the youngest person to pilot a plane across the country ended in twisted, fatal wreckage. In the aftermath of the tragedy, the previously exploitative media began its calls for more responsibility by parents and other authorities. Into this breast-beating fest stepped her mother, one Lisa Hathaway, a self-proclaimed New Age healer whose maunderings under the circumstances took America's collective breath away. She, along with her late ex-husband, mangled in the plane crash, espoused a theory that the job of a parent was to stand on the sideline, exhorting the child to explore any and all whims, and that any strictures were abusive, paternalistic, antilife, and so on. "I would want all my children to die in a state of joy," she proclaimed within minutes of her child's death. She vowed to fight the FAA's move to toughen up rules about kids flying airplanes: "You look at Jess and tell me how you can question that. Have you seen a seven-year-old shine like that? She had room to be; she had room to have a life." Well, almost. (Ironically, most came away with the impression that Hathaway and the father had gone about creating and marketing Jessica and her stunt with the crassness and manipulations of old-time stage parents. These ol' hippies could have taught some tricks to the Culkins or to JonBenet Ramsey's folks.)

At the other extreme are cases where parental control of children has extended beyond the realm of what many, or even most, would consider appropriate. For example, courts have tackled the issue of whether Christian Scientists—whose religion rejects medical interventions, even to the point of abhorring the use of a thermometer, in favor of healing prayer—have the right to withhold medical care from their sick children. Some of these cases make for pretty painful reading, these tales of children dying excruciating deaths from readily cured diseases. The court decisions are clear: that may be fine for consenting adults, but parents cannot let a child die for lack of medical care, in the name of their religion.

The courts decided differently, however, when it came to a group of Amish parents in Wisconsin who wanted to keep their children out of high school—where, for the first time, they would be exposed to non-Amish classmates and so might be tempted to stray from their tight-knit community. The state argued, in part, that if Amish children were to become Amish adults, it should be out of knowledge and choice, not because they were sheltered extensions of their parents. But the U.S. Supreme Court ruled in favor of the parents.

So it's not okay for parents to kill their kids because of a belief system, but it's fine to leave them so uneducated and ill-prepared for the outside world as to give them no choice but to remain in the fold. Thus, Amish children not only "belong" to their parents, but to the Amish heritage as a whole. (And as discussed in the notes after this piece, the court went out of its way to say that this sort of decision only applies to religious heritages of the right sort—cults need not apply.)

A similar belief, in a very different setting, emerges from a story about Gandhi. As appalling violence raged between fanatic Hindu and Muslim nationalists, he commenced a fast to the death for peace. Huge crowds supporting peace converged around him in a vigil. At one point, a bloodstained Hindu fanatic bursts through the crowd to confess his sins to Gandhi: he has slaughtered an innocent Muslim family with his own hands. Gandhi instructs him on his path to redemption. Take a Muslim child, an orphan of this madness, and raise this child with every comfort you can provide . . . as an observant Muslim, as one of your enemies. An immensely moving prescription that made an entire nation sigh, premised on that notion—by dint of birth, this one belongs to the Muslims, and, thus, you must help facilitate his return to them.

Those debates have an abstract intellectual resemblance to the case of Jennifer Bush. But they pale as one begins to comprehend what happened to this child and, unfortunately, to others like her. In April 1996, Jennifer's mother, who had been appealing through the press for help with her daughter's astronomical medical bills, was arrested. Detective work by the police and child-welfare workers in

Florida, where the Bushes lived, showed that the cause of Jennifer's persistent infections was ultimately neither gene nor pathogen. The girl's symptoms, it seems, had been created by her mother. Incredibly, according to the charges, for which she was eventually convicted, Mom had been putting feces into Jennifer's feeding tubes. Plus, there was some major financial fiddling that was added to the charges. It even looked as if a letter to the Clintons, asking for help in a big, childlike scrawl, had been penned by a maternal ghostwriter.

Horrifying, stunning. And a disorder of parental behavior common enough to qualify as a syndrome.

The phenomenon is most commonly called Munchausen's by proxy. In 1951, a psychiatrist named Richard Asher described an odd disorder in which individuals fabricated symptoms to obtain needless medical care. Subspecies of this had already been noted and named, including "laparotomorphilia migrans" (fabrication of symptoms resulting in an operation), "neurologia phantastica" (fabrication of neurological symptoms), and "haemorrhagica histrionica" (self-induced blood loss). Asher, emphasizing the common theme, now gave them a single, unifying term, which he termed Munchausen's syndrome (named for Baron Karl von Münchhausen, an eighteenth-century German soldier who was known for telling tall tales about his adventures. For some reason, Asher dropped the second *h* in the name). Then in 1977, a British pediatrician named Roy Meadow, of St. James University Hospital in Leeds, formalized a relative of Munchausen's syndrome in which a parent fabricates symptoms in a child, logically terming it Munchausen's by proxy (MBP).

MBP is stunning, riveting, because of the social complexity of the disorder, the fact that the unimaginable behavior on the part of the parent typically winds up succeeding with the unwitting collaboration of medical authorities. But before delving into that, the mere case reports of what MBP is about are grist for nightmares.

In the less invasive versions of MBP, the parent merely manipulates samples taken from the child. Meadow's original paper described the case of a six-year-old girl admitted to the hospital with foul-smelling, bloody urine that teemed with bacteria, seemingly due to a massive urinogenital tract infection. Physicians in prior hospitals had seen her and were stumped, referring her to these experts. Oddities began to emerge. In the morning, there would be an infection with one type of bacteria. By the evening, that bacteria would have been vanquished, only to be replaced with an onslaught of a different one. Even stranger, in an afternoon's sample, there might be no bacteria at all. Increasingly powerful medications were given to the child, all for naught—the infection continued. Alert nurses noticed a pattern: there were bacteria in the samples only when the mother was around to help with collecting a urine sample, a pattern documented in Meadow's paper. Eventually, chemical analysis revealed that the blood in the urine was menstrual blood from the mother.

The really horrific quality is seen when a parent manipulates events going on *in* the child's body. Some MBP parents have been found to generate a mysterious rash in their child by rubbing caustic solutions into the skin. In another report, a mother of a two-year-old beat her daughter's ankles severely enough to generate severe inflammation that required incisions and drainage, then kept the area infected by contaminating the incisions with soil and coffee grounds. A pediatric cardiologist at the University of Cincinnati named Douglas Schneider and colleagues reported an even more invasive case. Most parents learn about syrup of ipecac somewhere along the way, the terrible, essential drug needed to purge a child who has swallowed some poison. And this mother was force-feeding her five-year-old son ipecac, triggering violent vomiting and diarrhea. Suspicious nurses found bottles of ipecac secreted in the hospital room, in the mother's coat pocket. The vomiting abruptly stopped after that, and the child recovered, merely with heart damage (a potential side effect of ipecac). The report describes an additional case in which a three-year-old, after vomiting six to eight times a day since birth, died.

Meadow, in his original paper, described another case, this time of a toddler whose salt balance was dramatically, incessantly out of balance, with far too much sodium in the bloodstream, a problem also there since birth. As per the usual pattern, the problem disappeared whenever the mother was kept away from the child. A trained nurse who was skilled at using a gastric feeding tube, she was apparently force-feeding salt to her son. He died as social services personnel were planning his protective custody. And in a truly horrifying case, a University of Chicago pediatrician named Edward Seferian reported on a six-year-old boy whose body had been invaded by a menagerie of bacteria. This was rare, puzzling—one seldom sees a child who is so immunosuppressed that the body festers with polymicrobial sepsis. But the mystery deepened—the child's immune system wasn't suppressed, it was functioning just fine. Yet wave after wave of bacterial infection occurred in the blood, accompanied by sustained high fevers, all resistant to a pharmacy's worth of antibiotics. Eventually, the staff became suspicious, and the father supplied some corroborating details that pointed to the mother, the mother who had become enough of a regular on the ward to help with the intravenous feeding of the child, the mother who had earlier worked as a medical technician and knew her way around a hospital, the mother who was ultimately found to be introducing feces into her child's bloodstream.

Here are the techniques available to the MBP parent: Bleeding can be fabricated by adding outside blood or can be induced with enough anticoagulants to turn a scratch into a river. Seizures can be provoked by repeatedly pressing down on the carotid arteries in the neck. A torporous state of central nervous system depression can be induced by insulin injections. Apnea severe enough to be convincingly recorded on a breathing monitor can be induced with smothering. Diarrhea can be induced with laxatives or salt poisoning, vomiting with emetics like ipecac.

And here are the most common drugs and poisons force-fed to the children to generate symptoms: anticonvulsants, opiates, tranquilizers, antidepressants, salt, antihistamines, and, of course, laundry bleach.

The average perpetrator is, overwhelmingly, the mother (and this is sufficiently so that I will write throughout as if this were solely the case—this is just an expository convenience). The average victim is under six years of age, certainly in no position to tell anyone that when no one is around, Mommy injects a finely suspended filtrate of dog shit into her child. The average lag time between the child's entrée into the medical system and discovery is fifteen months, ample time for those serious and recalcitrant symptoms to generate plenty of tests and scans, for a round of medication, for a more powerful second medication, for that new experimental third medication, for feeding tubes, drainage lines, transfusions, urinary catheters, enemas, IV lines, and endless injections, even for repeated anesthetizations and surgeries. And the mortality rate approaches 10 percent.

One gropes for a way to understand this, to tie these obscenities to some sort of explanation, as if MBP were a maddened extension of something remotely familiar. But many of these potential links are severed because of what MBP is not. This is not child abuse in the (tragic that the following word will be understood) "everyday" sense of, say, beating the child. That typically involves active effort on the perpetrator's part to avoid prying medical authorities, in contrast to the situation with MBP. This is not some maternal anxiety disorder, a mother so pathologically worried about her child's health as to fabricate problems so that the child can remain safely ensconced in the medical system. There appear to be no such anxieties. Nor is this something called "mothering to death," where the maternal anxiety about the child's health involves a dread avoidance of the medical system. It is not "masquerade syndrome," in which a mother will lie about a child's health to keep her out of school—in such cases, the motive is to extend the mothering, delay the child's independence, and there is typically complicity between the mother and child, and no actual illness induced.

As also defined, MBP cannot involve a delusional but sincere belief on the part of a parent that the child is sick. The parent doesn't believe that the baby repeatedly manages to swallow some poison, necessitating ipecac eight times a day. The parents don't believe that bleach, an occasional smothering, and feces under the skin drive out Satan. There are no whispering voices in the head insisting that they provoke seizures in their child.

And as a final version of what MBP is not, its manipulativeness cannot be for the goal of material gain—the mother tearfully begging the landlord to be understanding about the late rent check because, after all, her child is sick again. Insofar as there might be any material gain, it is a secondary motive, at best.

So what is the disease about? In MBP families, the husband is typically nonexistent or at least distant, and Meadow speculates that the fabricated drama, in the latter cases, is partially meant to pull in that disinterested husband. Another clue: as hinted at in the case reports, about half of MBP perpetrators have had some medical training. This is a prerequisite for the technical skill and the familiarity with hospital culture needed to pull off some of the fabrications. And Meadow noted a pattern subsequently reported by others: most of those mothers with medical backgrounds had *failed* at their medical careers; they had been nursing students who didn't cut it academically, physician's assistants fired for their emotional instability. Meadow writes, "It could be suggested that some [of the MBP mothers] were determined to defeat the system that had defeated them."

But the central, defining motivation in MBP is a desire to be utterly enveloped in the medical system. "Hospitals can be a strong (and dangerous) addiction," as Meadow puts it. MBP mothers devote themselves full-time to the child's illness and go weeks without leaving the ward. The medical staff initially views them as self-sacrificing saints. In return, they reap a sense of comfort and security, the almost sensual pleasure at the attention, the intertwining of nursing and being nursed, the acceptance into a rich, structured social community.

This insertion into the hospital setting is not merely presented as an energetic vigil for a sick child. The mother quickly inveigles her way into the community of the staff. Becoming a model "civilian" on the ward requires a manipulative social expertise that is even greater than the medical expertise that many of these MBP mothers have. The typical MBP mother is effusively complimentary of the staff, grateful, appreciative, trying gamely to be diplomatic about how much more capable everyone here is than those incompetents in that previous hospital. Within days, she is showing up with brownies for the night crew (in a high-brow version of this, one MBP mother turned out to be a primary fund-raiser for the hospital's pediatric ward). Soon, the mother has found out everyone's birthday, arrives with gifts that are just barely on the right side of being too personal. She becomes a confidante, hearing about nurses' romantic problems, the shared heartaches of parenthood. She figures out the politics and conflicts of the house staff, quietly letting someone know whose side she is on—theirs, of course. She understands. She understands the abuse nurses have to often put up with from the doctors, she understands the strain and insecurities the young doctors have to work under, so impressive in her ability to hear about other people's problems when she has so many of her own—"Do you know whose kid is hers? Yeah, the really sick one; it's amazing how strong and giving this woman is. . . ." She becomes more than an undefined ward mascot. Half the female staffers suspect they have found a new best friend; half the male staffers think they'll be in bed with her soon. An entire medical unit is seduced, ready to go the extra mile to help her mysteriously ill child, ready to accommodate the mother's desire to be in the thick of virtually every medical procedure, ready to suspend the slightest whisper of suspicion as absurd and unworthy.*

---

*This style of social manipulativeness shares many traits with "borderline personality disorder." Borderlines are notorious for chewing up inexperienced clinicians for breakfast. Grizzled mental-health elders, overseeing the training of young psychiatrists or psychologists, talk about the need for their young'uns to become "borderline-proof," hoping that the first such patient they encounter merely teaches them

This complex edifice of manipulation, that ability of the MBP mother to work her way into the social community of the staff, becomes a vicious spring trap when someone begins to suspect that the pieces aren't adding up. The features of the kid's illness begin to raise suspicions. Or maybe it's that the perfect mother never seems as concerned about her child as is the staff. Perhaps someone finally notices how the vomiting, the bacteria, the fever only seem to occur when the mother is around. Or maybe someone walks into the child's room and catches the tail end of the mother doing something behind closed curtains to the sobbing, agitated child. The sleuth is probably going to be a senior nurse, maybe the head nurse, who has some experience and jadedness about patients and their families. It's going to be someone who is distinctly borderline-proof, who is not looking for a best friend at work to pour out her heart to. It's going to be a no-nonsense type who is not prone to the touchy-feely and is probably not the most popular staffer.

The skeptic airs the suspicions, and the ward explodes into dissent, as most staffers turn on the skeptic. These are accusations against their new friend, against the most devoted mother any of them have ever

indelible clinical lessons, rather than destroying their career or personal life.

In mental-health lingo, *borderline* can be a hideously active verb: "Christ, I have to go waste the afternoon in a trumped-up disciplinary hearing for Smith, the second-year resident. Poor kid. He had this patient, smart, young professional, totally seductive style, gets Smith to start prescribing tons of Demerol for her for no reason. He finally figures it out, tries to stop her meds, and now she's got half the board convinced that he was trying to get into her pants during therapy sessions. And, naturally, turns out she's done this Demerol stunt at four other training clinics, but it's not admissible at his hearing because she keeps countercharging them into chickening out of putting it in her records. So now it's hit the fan for Smith. Poor kid, he got totally borderlined." The infamous Glenn Close character in *Fatal Attraction,* before she went postal with the knives and the bunny, had many borderline traits. Masters of manipulation, emotionally labile, capable of grandiose suicidal gestures (but rarely of true suicidalism), functioning in a black-and-white world of villains or idealized heroes, with relationships that are usually transient and superficial because they can't survive that sort of dichotomizing, borderlines possess an all-consuming surface persona of control and duplicity that makes one wonder who, if anyone, is inside.

seen. Terry Foster, clearly a battle-wearied senior nurse, writes in the nursing journal *RN* about how manipulative individuals such as these can "split" an entire staff. Most nurses are unaware of these sorts of disorders, find it unimaginable that such a thing can exist, as it runs counter to the core of the caregiving of their profession. Doctors, who are usually as psychologically sophisticated as an adolescent candy striper, find the accusations by some abrasive, unpopular nurse against this personable, committed individual to be ludicrous. Foster writes about how the doctors don't even show up at the staff meetings called about the matter.

How can any of these mothers get away with it, often for such fatally long periods? The borderline style is obviously a big part of it. Moreover, in most pediatric wards, parents are encouraged to spend as much time there as possible, and to be active participants in health care—generally a good thing, but open to the depredations of wolves in mother's clothing. Part is because physicians are suckers for exotic, complicated cases that challenge them, and they lose the forest for the trees—a medical system that is "specialized, investigation-oriented, fascinated by rare conditions, often ignorant of abusive behaviors, and too accepting of reported histories," according to Terence Donald and Jon Jureidini, two Australian pediatricians who have written about MBP.

But there is a darker reason too. By the time the first jaundiced accusations emerge, every health-care professional has been complicit, albeit unwillingly and unconsciously, in what was done to that healthy child. The injections, the blood draws, the drainage incisions, the enemas, the surgeries. The restraining of the sobbing, frightened child for a procedure. The pain. "All for the child's own good." All for nothing.

Donald and Jureidini write about the "systems" aspects of MBP with particular insight. Throughout the literature, there is confusion about whether the MBP label describes the perpetrating mother or the victimized child—many in the field write as if the diagnosis somehow floats between the two actors. Donald and Jureidini take that floating sense a step further. MBP "best describes a complex *transaction* among at least three persons—a parent, her or his child, and the physician" (their emphasis). The formal definition of MBP requires the needless treatment on the part of the medical system. Given the gradual process by which suspicions typically emerge, it seems impossible for the most caring of practitioners not to feel sullied and guilty. And, as such, MBP is probably the diagnosis that everyone is most invested in not making.

The strangest and most fascinating aberrancies of human behavior are the perversions of our strongest emotions. We all have our moments of imagined violence, spittle-flecked fantasies of explosive, visceral aggression. Thus, it becomes that much more incomprehensible when some murderer kills with an affectless, reptilian coldness. We all know something about the warm, limbic glow of love. Thus, Jeffrey Dahmer becomes that much more boggling when, in addition to murdering, dismembering, and cannibalizing his victims, he spoke of "loving" them as well.

And we all know something about maternalism, and here is the most boggling inversion of that imaginable. How could they do it, how could they do it to their own flesh and blood?

And here is where we return to how this piece began, an exploration of what boundaries there are, if any, to parents' concept of "their own." In some MBP cases the perpetrators seem to be sheer, brutal exploiters. Such people have an intense need for the attention of the medical system and have discovered that a sick child is a wonderful entrée to it. If the rewards of attention were the same, that kind of MBP mother would just as readily lie to a veterinarian about the symptoms of her goldfish, or to the people at Sears about the clock radio that stops working. Child as object, child as pawn. In these cases, the criminality of the acts seems to vastly outweigh the implied illness behind the acts.

But in some cases, something much more complex is going on. A number of studies have reported that in most MBP mothers, there is also Munchausen's on the part of the mother herself. Maybe the mother was cured of her Munchausen's once the child was born and the MBP began. Maybe the Munchausen's began only when the MBP was discovered and prevented. Maybe they are concurrent, beginning with the mother damaging both of them when one was pregnant and the other a fetus. Meadow writes about cases where there is virtual "transmission" of fabricated symptoms between mother and child.

That picture is completely different from the one that sees the child as clock radio. Here is a vastly sick, intimate intertwining of mother and child, with a complete failure of ego boundaries, a pathological view of the child as an extension of the parent, a confusion as to what constitutes, literally, one's own flesh and blood.

And it is that intertwining that is ultimately the most disturbing thing about MBP, because it contains a glimmer of familiarity. Both Meadow and Marc Feldman, a psychiatrist at the University of Alabama, draw parallels between MBP and the subtler ego-boundary problems that all parents have, this quandary of how much a child is a vessel for your values and beliefs, hopes and disappointments. There is an invitation to irrationality when you hold your child for the first time, when you realize that this is someone who will likely be there long after you are gone, and whose person will someday, you believe, constitute a partial biography of you.

ᴏ NOTES AND FURTHER READING ᴏ

This piece has had a strange emotional pull for me. I had been fascinated with Munchausen's syndrome for years and had only vaguely been aware of MBP—oh, yeah, sometimes people fabricate symptoms in their kid instead of in themselves, weird. Then my first child was born, and about five days later, drifting back to sleep after the umpteenth awakening in the middle of the night, I was suddenly catapulted into utter alertness with the thought *My God, there's a disease where a parent intentionally generates illnesses in a child, where they intentionally <u>hurt</u> their baby.* I instantly had a frantic need to read everything available on the subject and, ultimately, to write and write about it—it's that professorial instinct of thinking that if you cogitate on a subject long enough, if you lecture on it sufficiently, it will eventually give up and go away. Thus, this will be a particularly long stretch of notes reflecting, in part, how much verbiage I forced myself to cut out of the piece itself.

The initial phases of the Jennifer Bush case were covered in *Newsweek,* April 29, 1996. The story of her mother's conviction by a jury in Broward County, Florida, after a mere seven hours of deliberation, is covered in the October 7, 1999, *Sun-Sentinel* of South Florida.

Thomas Szasz's thinking is summarized in books of his such as *The Myth of Mental Illness* (2nd ed., New York: Perennial Editions, 1984) or *Ideology and Insanity* (New York: Anchor Books, 1970).

The death of Jessica Dubroff, and the quotes from Lisa Hathaway, came from both *Time* and *Newsweek,* April 22, 1996.

The definitive case regarding the rights of Christian Science parents is *The People v. Rippberger,* 231 CalApp 3d 1667: 283 Cal Rpter, July 1991. Eight-month-old Natalie Middleton-Rippberger contracted bacterial meningitis, complete with apparent high fever (estimated, since her Christian Science parents would not use a thermometer) and heavy convulsions. The parents sought no conventional medical care, instead seeking assistance from a Christian Science nurse, who advised the parents to keep the child warm and nourished as well as to notify a Christian Science committee that prayers for the child were not working as quickly as should be expected. After Natalie's apparently excruciating death, which could readily have been prevented, her parents were charged with felony child endangerment.

The Supreme Court decision regarding mandatory schooling requirements for Amish children is found in *State of Wisconsin v.*

Yoder, 70–110, 1972. Based on their desire to shield their children from the influences of non-Amish culture in high school, a couple named Yoder kept their kids out of school. They were cited and fined. Just to show how much everyone involved knew this was about principles, the fine was $5, and the Yoders appealed; the case eventually landed in the Supreme Court.

The attorney for Wisconsin emphatically expressed respect and admiration for the Amish, but argued that the state had a vested interest in making sure kids got educated, and that eight years of school did not equal the required ten years. He emphasized high school as an ideal place for socialization and choice, exactly the things the parents feared. The attorney for the Amish, in turn, discussed how successful the Amish were, what natural educators they were with their approach of teaching by doing, and how sending kids to two years of high school would destroy this fragile minority culture. The wise black robes deliberated and came up with a ruling that strikes this legal neophyte as weird as hell.

In the majority opinion, the justices started off by praising the Amish educational system: "The evidence showed that the Amish provide continuing informal vocational education to their children designed to prepare them for life in the rural Amish community." They then said that Wisconsin's argument about eight years of education leaving a child ill-prepared to deal with the outside world was weakened by the fact that the Amish didn't leave the community much anyway. They didn't seem to note a tautology: of course few leave the Amish community when their education has only prepared them to be Amish. There was no discussion about what happened to the people who did leave the community. Nor of what the kids in this particular case wanted. None raised the question of whether a minority culture that was so fragile as to be destroyed by two years of secular high school deserved to be preserved as a museum piece. Concepts like "rights of children" or "freedom of choice" were notably absence in the majority opinion.

As noted, the court came down in favor of the Amish—their kids could be kept out of school past the eighth grade—and in a truly odd way. First, the court explained why two fewer years of schooling wouldn't harm the kids. Keeping the kids out of school "will not impair the physical or mental health of the child" . . . nor get in the way of such children discharging "the duties and responsibilities of citizenship." Furthermore, in case Amish children did happen to leave the community at some point, "There is no specific evidence that . . . upon leaving the Amish community, Amish children . . . would become burdens on society . . . or in any other way materially detract from the welfare of society." Cool criteria. I'd definitely be satisfied if my children got only enough schooling to be ensured of not being mentally ill or driving down the gross national product.

The justices then carefully limited the boundaries of their decision. First, they stated that you couldn't keep your kids out of school based on a minority philosophy, only a minority religion—they explicitly said that Thoreau couldn't have gotten away with this. Next, they made it clear that they weren't talking about all religions deserving this protection. This was 1971, and they went out of their way to warn hippie cult religions not to even think of starting any tomfoolery. "It cannot be overemphasized that we are not dealing with a way of life and mode of education by a group claiming to have *recently* discovered some *progressive* or more *enlightened* process for rearing children for modern life" (my emphases). So the Moonies and Krishnas can't keep their kids from going out for the cheerleading squad.

The incident with Gandhi is described in Collins L and Lapierre D, *Freedom at Midnight* (New York: Acacia, 1997).

The source of the *Munchausen* in Munchausen's syndrome, and MBP: It all started with the eighteenth-century Baron von Münchhausen (who came with two *h*'s, in contrast to his namesake disease). A nobleman soldier, he fought the Turks in the Russo-Turkish war of 1737 before spending his remaining years entertaining guests at his estate with tales of war ventures and sportsmanship. The standard story is that Münchhausen was a tiresome blowhard with his stories, and that someone ultimately published a collection of them that came to be viewed as the epitome of confabulatory, impossible tales of self-congratulatory derring-do. According to one revisionist historian bent on clearing the name of the poor baron, the guy's stories were actually factual, and the anonymous author—some powdered-wig ex-houseguest with a grudge, intent on embarrassing the baron and apparently succeeding—was the one who conflated. (Small-world department: Münchhausen was apparently cuckolded in his later years by a younger wife, who was able to escape to her trysts thanks to her skills at faking a chronic illness, necessitating convalescing at a spa.) All this is described in Haddy R, "The Münchhausen of Munchausen syndrome: a historical perspective," *Archives of Family Medicine* 2 (1993): 141.

Meadow's original paper on MBP is Meadow R, "Munchausen syndrome by proxy: the hinterland of child abuse," *Lancet* 2 (1997): 343. The case involving beating of ankles is found in Bryk M and Siegel P, "My mother caused my illness: the story of a survivor of Munchausen by proxy syndrome," *Pediatrics* 100 (1997): 1. The ipecac case is found in Schneider D et al., "Clinical and pathologic aspects of cardiomyopathy from ipecac administration in Munchausen's syndrome by proxy," *Pediatrics* 97 (1996): 902. The case involving feces in the IV line: Seferian E, "Polymicrobial bacteremia: a presentation of Munchausen syndrome by proxy," *Clinical Pediatrics* (July 1997): 419.

The characteristics of the MBP parent and child, and the range of symptoms induced in MBP, can be found in McClure R, Davis P, Meadow S, and Sibert J, "Epidemiology of Munchausen syndrome by proxy, nonaccidental poisoning, and nonaccidental suffocation," *Archives of Diseases of Children* 75 (1996): 57; Rosenberg D, "Web of deceit: a literature review of Munchausen syndrome by proxy," *Child Abuse and Neglect* 11 (1987): 547; Meadow, "Munchausen syndrome by proxy"; and Feldman M, Rosenquist P, and Bond J, "Concurrent factitious disorder and factitious disorder by proxy. Double jeopardy," *General Hospital Psychiatry* 19 (1997): 24. Reliable statistics on MBP are not available, and indeed, the precise criteria for making a clinical diagnosis are still evolving. Along with the growing awareness and diagnosis of this tragic disorder, there is also the tragic circumstance of false accusations of MBP.

What MBP is not is discussed in Meadow R, "What is, and what is not, Munchausen syndrome by proxy?" *Archives of Diseases of Children,* 72 (1995): 534; also, Feldman, Rosenquist, and Bond, "Concurrent factitious disorder."

The social manipulations and borderline features of MBP mothers run throughout the MBP literature cited. Foster's writing about how MBP mothers can divide an entire medical staff is found in Foster T, "Munchausen's syndrome? We've met it head on," *RN,* August 17, 1996. The vulnerability of medical staffers to MBP deception, and the triadic nature of MBP, is written about in Donald T and Jureidini J, "Munchausen syndrome by proxy: child abuse in the medical system," *Archives of Pediatric and Adolescent Medicine* 150 (1996): 753.

The co-occurrence of MBP and Munchausen's syndrome was first discussed in Meadow R, "Munchausen syndrome by proxy," *Archives of Diseases of Childhood* 57 (1982): 92, and has been noted in many of the other papers cited.

One of the most ornate and horrifying of MBP cases, too lengthy to put into the main essay, is that of Waneta Hoyt and Alfred Steinschneider, covered at length on May 5–7, 1996, in the *Syracuse Post-Standard.* A young woman living outside Syracuse, New York, in the 1960s and '70s, Hoyt had suffered the indescribable pain of having a series of her infants die of sudden infant death syndrome (SIDS). A young pediatrician at Upstate Medical Center at Syracuse, Steinschneider was on the rise as a researcher for his advocacy that SIDS was caused by apnea, a mysterious cessation of breathing. Hoyt had been sent to his clinic with her fourth child. The three previous had died from SIDS, and the fourth was already in trouble—Hoyt reported the same pattern emerging at home at night, the child having terrifying episodes of apnea, requiring resuscitation, vigorous stimulation to get her breathing again. This seemed strongly confirmatory of Steinschneider's theory about the critical role played by apnea in SIDS, namely that the neurons in the brain stem that regulate automatic breathing during sleep can be immature in their function in some infants, can cease working for long, fatal periods. Such immaturity was viewed by Steinschneider as having a biological flavor to it—an intrinsic flaw in the system—and that SIDS could run in a family such as Hoyt's seemed to support his idea. These poor children carried an inborn biological weakness that made a peaceful night's sleep chancing death.

Fortunately, Steinschneider was on the cutting edge of his science, and Molly Hoyt became the first child cared for at home with an apnea monitoring machine, newly developed by the doctor. The idea was that no parent could spend all of each night standing vigil, in case the child stopped breathing. The machine would, instead, stand watch, sounding an alarm at each episode of apnea, so that the parent could rush in and resuscitate the child. It worked flawlessly for Molly, documenting that she had apneic episodes virtually nightly, just as Waneta Hoyt had reported. Hoyt would use the machine as an indicator of when to stimulate Molly and would bring her to the hospital at times when the clusters of episodes became too much for her to handle. Aided by the machine, she was able to keep the child going for some months until the terrible weakness of those breathing centers in the brain finally triumphed: Molly died at home at close to three months of age, as her mother worked frantically to jump-start her breathing reflexes with mouth-to-mouth resuscitation. A year later, Hoyt and her husband had a fifth child, Noah, and had to endure the unbearable cycle again—an infant prone to severe clusters of apnea, the middle-of-the-night panic of resuscitation as the monitor's alarm signaled yet another breathing crisis, until, finally, the biology won again, another dead child at two months of age.

The cases of Molly and Noah were the centerpieces of Steinschneider's landmark 1972 paper and subsequent career. For about a decade after that, sleep apnea became the dominant paradigm for understanding SIDS, and Steinschneider was its most acclaimed champion. He rose in the professorial ranks, was eventually lured to a more prestigious university, eventually even had his own institute funded by grateful donors. During that ten-year stretch, Steinschneider received nearly one-quarter of all the funds spent by the federal government for SIDS research, something on the order of $5 million—this is a staggering dominance of a research field by a single investigator. And amid documentation by Steinschneider that his apnea monitor had cut the SIDS death rate in the Syracuse region since its introduction, sales flourished.

But, naturally, something was not quite right.

As usual, it began with a perceptive nurse attuned to human behavior rather than to medical reports. Something just didn't seem right about Waneta Hoyt. She was gregarious enough with the staff, but she was cold, aloof from the children, seemed far less concerned about them than did the nurses. Steinschneider later defended Hoyt, writing that her distancing was a protective mechanism. But there were more problems. The home-monitoring machine clearly did not work well, and it was impossible to distinguish between true apnea and one of the frequent false alarms due to glitches in the system. Maybe these babies weren't really having such frequent episodes of apnea? Most important, staff soon keyed in on the critical indicator that something was wrong: Molly and Noah never had apnea in the hospital. No apnea, no need to resuscitate, no need to stimulate to get the breathing started again. It was only at home. When Noah was sent home, nurses wept openly, predicting that Hoyt would kill him. And he was dead the next day.

Hoyt was not heard from again on that ward. Meanwhile, Steinschneider's theory was the dominant explanation for SIDS through-out the 1970s. But by the mid-1980s, things were shifting. Blue-ribbon panels of pediatricians—one organized by the American Academy of Pediatrics, another by the National Institutes of Health—concluded that the home monitors were useless for preventing SIDS. And it became apparent that Steinschneider's oft-repeated procla-mation about his monitor cutting the SIDS rate in Syracuse was non-sense—the SIDS rate had dropped in many other cities without the use of Steinschneider's monitors.

In 1994, an eager, skeptical district attorney in New York State decided to pursue the Hoyt case. Within hours of being picked up for questioning, Waneta Hoyt confessed to murdering all five by smothering.

At her trial, medical records were introduced showing that there had never been any apnea requiring resuscitation for a Hoyt child in the hospital; any such episodes were exclusively reported by Hoyt at home. Nurses said that there had never been any apnea in the hospital. Steinschneider, testifying for the defense, insisted that such episodes had occurred, just as he had reported in his 1972 paper. When did those supposed episodes occur, who were the attending nurses? He couldn't remember. Did he know of any records that indicated that there were episodes of apnea in the hospital? He couldn't recollect any, but noted that things occurred that may not have been noted in the charts. As reported in the *Syracuse Post-Standard,* after the jury con-victed Hoyt, Steinschneider "suggested her confession was coerced."

Waneta Hoyt's motives remain a bit murky. At her confession, she claimed she had smothered the children because they would not stop crying. Were that the case, such impulsive violence would not qualify as MBP. However, the placid personality of the children, as reported by nurses, the pattern of repeated smotherings during a night, the gravitation toward the attention of medical authorities (rather than the nervous avoidance of it), all argue against that motive. Nurses who observed Hoyt at that time emphasized, instead, how she seemed to crave the attention she got because of the unique, tragic nature of her situation, suggesting that the actual deaths were due to smotherings that had gone too far—a definitive MBP profile. And naturally, one wonders whether Steinschneider's motives had something to do with the power and prestige this landmark study gained him in the medical community. And thus, in Dr. Steinschneider, we contemplate here the possibility of a supremely rare case of Munchausen by proxy by proxy.

PART III

Society and Who We Are

Introduction

On occasion, I wonder what sort of person I'd be like if they hadn't left. Between 1905 and the First World War, all the branches of my family made it out of Russia, and this occurred with a number of near misses—the train that almost left without my grandfather, the border guard who began to but then forgot to check the nonexistent papers. It could so easily have turned out otherwise, and then I'd be there. Would I have, as an adolescent, heaped the same contempt on Brezhnev as I did on Nixon? Instead of being an American model of one type of academic—Birkenstocks, teetotaling vegetarian, jeans—would I be a Slavic model—chain-smoking, vodka-laden, ill-fitting Polish-made suit, and an obsession with wheat genetics or topology? Maybe I wouldn't even be an academic. Would I be a peddler in some frostbitten hamlet, married to someone renowned for her skill at making a meal out of turnips and potatoes?

America is one big version of The Alternative Universe, thanks to emigration. Fisherman in the Mekong Delta or dot-commer in Silicon Valley? Wife of a camel herder in Rajasthan or family practitioner/weekend softball-league ace in Houston? At the core of this what-ifing is a key fact—we are shaped by the sort of society in which we live, and we would not be the same person if we had grown up elsewhere. The language you are raised with will constrain your patterns of thought (a finding that has floated around anthropology and linguistics for close to a century). The economic structure of your society will influence whether you tend to cooperate or cheat in formal game-theory settings, as recent research has shown. The marriage structure of a culture will help determine whether the most salient thought of, say, a man during his marriage ceremony is *This is the person with whom I will share love for the rest of my life, in whose arms I will die someday* or *Fourteen cows for a third wife? Damn, I think I got ripped off.* And the theology, myths, and urban legends of your civilization will shape how you think about some of the most fundamental questions in life—for example, is life intrinsically beautiful, or sinful?

And if the culture in which we live shapes who we are—our thoughts, emotions, and actions—it must shape our underlying biology as well. This can be for utterly obvious reasons—the culture you live in determines the diet you are exposed to, the medical care you receive, the physicality with which you earn your daily bread. But the culture/biology link can be more direct and fundamental than that. As but one example, consider child development. The Cornell anthropologist Merideth Small looks at child-rearing practices from across the planet in her book *Our Babies, Ourselves.* You begin by reading her book assuming it is going to be an assortment box of prescriptions, that at the end you'll emerge with a perfect combo for your kids, a mixture of the Kwakiutl Baby Diet, the Trobriand Sleeping Program, and the Ituri Pygmy Infant Aerobics Plan. But, Small emphasizes, there is no perfect, "natural" program. Societies raise their children so that they grow into adults who behave in a way valued by that society, and thus they differ enormously on a variety of measures: In a particular culture, how often is a child typically held by parents, by nonparents? Do babies ever sleep alone and, if so, starting at what age? What is the average length of time that a child cries before it is picked up and comforted? And a massive literature now demonstrates that variables such as these will influence the development of the brain—for example, some recent work by Michael Meaney and colleagues at McGill University shows the precise mechanisms by which different styles of rodent mothering (yes, some rats are more attentive and nurturing moms than others) will differentially activate certain genes in the brains of their pups for the rest of their lives.

The final section of this book explores these ideas, in three forms: First, your society, and your place in your society, will influence your biology. Next, societies differ in how people think about the biology of their behaviors. Finally, biological factors, such as the ecosystem in which people dwell, will shape the sort of society they form.

Essay thirteen, "How the Other Half Heals," considers the first idea, looking at how your place in society influences the sort of diseases your body succumbs to. It has long been known that being poor, of low socioeconomic status, puts you more at risk for a huge number of diseases in all Westernized societies. This essay explores the smaller subset of diseases that are more common among the wealthy, with an ironic punch line. Essay fourteen, "The Cultural Desert," examines how ecology shapes theology and argues that the cultures that have come to dominate this planet, generating something akin to a world culture, are, thanks to ecology, some of the least appealing around.

Essay fifteen, "Monkeyluv," looks at the vagaries of passion and sexual attraction in a nonhuman primate society. Essay sixteen, "Revenge Served Warm," examines a key issue in evolutionary biology, namely how societies (human or otherwise) develop systems of cooperation. As will be shown, a direct and laudable route for this to happen is highly unlikely, but a more emotionally frothy and disquieting one is more plausible.

Essay seventeen, "Why We Want Their Bodies Back," looks at cross-cultural differences in how people think about the body, namely the body of someone dead. It was prompted by a very personal event, a mystery, a disappearance of two friends when I was in high school, and its only partial resolution, more than a quarter century later.

And finally, essay eighteen, "Open Season," considers a question that, with each passing year, becomes of more interest to me as a scientist, writer, and social mammal. A hallmark of culture is the generation of new things, whether in ideas, art, or technology. Why is it that, as we get older, we're less and less open to such novelty, and more drawn to the familiar and repetitive? Why is it that, once we pass a surprisingly young age, we become suckers for buying those "best of" anthologies of music from our adolesence, advertised on late-night TV?

How the Other Half Heals

M odern science has finally provided some information that
should aid all of us in making our lifestyle decisions. If you
wish to live a long and healthy life, it is far more advisable to be
wealthy than to be poor. Let's be more specific: try not to be born into
poverty, and if you have inadvertently made that mistake, change your
station in life ASAP.

People have long known about what is called the "socioeconomic
status (SES) gradient" in health. For example, in the United States, the
poorer you are, the more likely you are to get and to succumb to heart
disease, respiratory disorders, ulcers, rheumatoid disorders, psychiatric
diseases, or a number of types of cancer. And this is a whopper of an
effect—SES accounts for at least a five-to-ten-year spread of life
expectancies, and in some cases, disease or mortality risk increases
more than tenfold as you go from the wealthiest to the poorest seg-
ments of our society, with things worsening each step of the way.

Naturally, there's been some pretty energetic theorizing and investigating as to what this gradient is about.

A first obvious possibility is the issue of health-care access. Poor
people are less able to afford preventative health measures, regular
checkups, or the finest care that money can buy when something is
wrong. That should explain a lot of what is going on. But it turns out
that it doesn't. There are robust SES health gradients in genteel, egal-
itarian Scandinavian countries, as there were in the old Soviet work-

ers' paradise (although to lesser extents in both cases than in sweaty, capitalistic Amerika). Furthermore, the SES gradient *worsened* in the United Kingdom over the twentieth century, despite the establishment of universal health care. And finally, the SES gradient is just as clear for a number of diseases whose prevalence are independent of preventative measures or health-care access. When it comes to these diseases (such as juvenile diabetes), you could go to the doctor for preventative checkups three times a day and, just for good measure, get centrifuged every Saturday, and that still wouldn't change your risk. So much for limited health-care access as *the* cause of the SES gradient.

Another obvious factor contributing to the gradient is that the poor have too many health risks and too few health-promoting factors in their lives. This can be quite substantial. The poor are more likely to smoke, drink to excess, and to be obese. And there are also uneven distributions of living near toxic waste dumps, working in dangerous industrial occupations, being surrounded by gang warfare, on the one hand, and health-club memberships, pesticide-free veggies, and stress-reducing hobbies on the other. Yet major risk factors and protective factors of lifestyle account for only a third of the variability in the SES gradient.

Education is thought to play a role as well. Number of years of schooling is an extremely reliable correlate of SES status, raising the possibility that part of the poor health of the poor has to do with ignorance about health care and risks. Indeed, studies have shown that poorly educated people are less likely to be able to follow a complex drug regime, understand the results of something like a Pap test, or to have heard of the startling fact that smoking is not good for you. And, remarkably, new medical advances often worsen the SES gradient, simply because it is the better educated who hear about these advances, understand their significance, and understand how to access them. But despite this, education can't be the main explanation of the SES health gradient, simply because the gradient still exists for diseases against which no stack of diplomas will protect you.

Faced with findings such as these, most in the field have come to believe that the SES gradient is predominantly about psychosocial factors—in other words, mostly about the stress of poverty. If you think that fighting your way up the corporate ladder is stressful, try having the ladder supported on your back. Psychological stress is built around a lack of control, predictability, outlets, and social support, and the poor are awash in those—layoffs whenever the economy winds down, the chance that the slumlord won't turn on the heat just yet, the vacation that can never be afforded, and with everyone so damn tired from working two jobs, a "social support network" being yuppie jargon. And in support of this, it is diseases that are thought to be most sensitive to stress that have the steepest SES gradients (such as psychiatric disorders and heart disease). Further support for the stress connection comes from some tremendously important recent work. While objective SES is a good predictor of various measures of health, often an even better predictor is *subjective* SES—in other words, the most important thing is not *being* poor. It's *feeling* poor. And as another body of key research shows, in a place like the United States, feeling poor usually means being *made* to feel poor—high degrees of income inequality, poverty amid plenty.

While researchers continue to understand the nuances of what causes the SES health gradient, what is undeniable is its existence and magnitude. Here's a dramatic example of it: In one study, the health of a group of elderly nuns was examined. These women had lived together for decades, with the same medical care, diet, exposure to health dangers, and benefits. And remarkably, disease patterns and longevity were predicted by the SES of these women when they became nuns in their youth, half a century before. Whatever the gradient's causes, poverty leaves a hell of a persistent health scar.

So again, some useful advice—try to be wealthy if you want to decrease the likelihood of most diseases. Most, but as it turns out, not all. A few diseases show an *inverse* SES gradient, where it is the wealthy that are more likely to get them. These diseases teach us a few

149

things about society, the nature of illness, and, as the main point of this piece, the occasional dangers of the best medical science that money can buy.

In some cases, no one has a clue as to why a disease is more common among the wealthy. One example is an autoimmune disease, where your immune system accidentally considers a part of your body to be an alien invader and attacks it. A number of autoimmune diseases, such as rheumatoid arthritis (in which your joints are attacked), show the classic SES gradient of the poor getting hammered. But to everyone's utter puzzlement, an inverse gradient exists for multiple sclerosis, where a part of the nervous system comes under immune attack.

For a few diseases, there are logical explanations for the inverse SES pattern. In his *Theory of the Leisure Class,* the sociologist Thorstein Veblen wrote about the symbols of indolent wealth in different societies. In imperial China, it was useless, bound feet. In the newly settled American West, if a rancher was sufficiently wealthy, he could afford to let some of his grazing land lie fallow and would make sure the land was conspicuously near his house, so that guests could marvel—the invention of the lawn (Veblen, unfortunately, did not live long enough to have the chance to incorporate plastic lawn flamingos into his thinking). For the wealthy nineteenth-century urbanite, the Veblenian symbol of healthful leisure was alabaster white skin. Time and society change, and at least until recently, a year-round tan had become a sign of rotisseried privilege—beach houses, ski trips, and tennis courts. As it turns out, melanoma currently shows an inverse SES gradient. People who actually *work* in the sun don't get alluring whole-body tans. They get red necks. Or, as is even more often the case, they don't get tanned much at all, given that farm workers in this country usually have a lot more melanin in their skin than do the models in ads for tanning salons.

In some cases, an inverse SES gradient is due to the glitch of its being easier to detect some versions of a disease more readily than others. Polio was long considered to be a disease of the better-off—catch a chill while yachting and you've got FDR in a wheelchair. Theodore Pincus of Vanderbilt Medical School has written about how this is a distortion. In actuality, the poor, typically living in much higher population densities, would contract the polio virus readily, often in the first months of life. But the key thing is that polio causes only mild and transient respiratory problems in a newborn. The poor really did get more polio. They simply got it under conditions where it wasn't detected as such.

The primatologist Craig Packer of the University of Minnesota has reported what I consider to be a similar example of a spurious inverse SES disease . . . among baboons. Baboons don't have socioeconomic status, but they sure have social status, namely dominance ranks. Being a low-ranking baboon has much in common with being a poor Westernized human, including having a disproportionate share of both physical and psychological stressors. A number of scientists, including myself, have found signs of worse health among low-ranking primates, including more stress hormones in the bloodstream, crummy immune systems, and higher blood pressure. Unexpectedly, Packer and colleagues reported an inverse gradient for miscarriages, in that higher-ranking females had the highest rate. Some colleagues of mine and I have suggested a detection problem similar to that with polio. Among the wild baboons that Packer studied, you cannot tell that a female is pregnant until she is in her second trimester (when the skin around her perineum takes on a distinctive color). Thus, by definition, this was not a case of detecting more miscarriages among higher-ranking females. This was detecting more second- or third-trimester miscarriages, something very different. Laboratory studies have shown that most primate miscarriages occur during the first trimester and are the ones that are the most stress-sensitive (as opposed to later miscarriages, which are more often related to genetic abnormalities or placental malfunction). Thus, we suggested that it is really lower-ranking females who have most of the miscarriages, but that it is simply not possible to detect this with a wild population. Not surprisingly, the two sides in this debate disagree with invigorating gusto.

But the inverse SES disease that I find to be most instructive is for real and occurs for a logical reason. It is a pediatric disease called hospitalism. It is now mostly a disease of the past, but that it ever existed constitutes an astounding and worrisome bit of medical history.

To begin to make sense of hospitalism, one must consider that in numerous traditional societies, newborns are not given names until they are a number of months or years old. This explanation is because of extremely high infant-mortality rates—wait until the child has actually managed to survive before personifying it with a name. A similar cultural adaptation could have existed early in the twentieth century in American foundling homes, institutions for abandoned or orphaned children. This was because of their staggeringly high mortality rates. In 1915, one physician, Henry Chapin, canvassed ten such places in the United States and reported numbers that didn't require a statistician to be detected—in all but one institution, every child died before two years of age. *Every child.* One does not even know what to do with the sadness of this datum, reading Chapin's stiff, mannered words some ninety years later.

And the situation at the time for children in hospitals was only somewhat less horrific. A typical child hospitalized for more than two weeks would start to show the signs of hospitalism—a listless wasting-away despite adequate food intake. Hospitalism involved weakening of muscles and loss of reflexes, and greatly increased risk of gastrointestinal and lung infections. With everything combined, mortality rates had gone up almost tenfold with the onset of hospitalism.

The savants had their guesses. Hospitals back then were dangerously unhealthy places to be, and the assumption was that with kids crammed in on pediatric wards, something infectious would be contracted. In Chapin's era, the gastrointestinal problems got the most attention. By a decade or so later, the pulmonary problems, particularly pneumonia, were the focus. All sorts of fancy terms emerged to describe such "marantic" infants, but everyone missed the boat as to what hospitalism was about.

We now know. Hospitalism lay at the intersection of two ideas at the time—a worship of sterile, aseptic conditions at all costs, and the belief among the (overwhelmingly male) pediatric establishment that touching, holding, and nurturing infants was sentimental maternal foolishness.

Children should be seen and not heard, and if you spare the rod, you spoil the child. So the sayings used to go. While early-twentieth-century America had, for the most part, moved beyond the grim world of child labor in sweatshops, most experts' notions of appropriate child-rearing would be considered cold and austere by today's standards. The first decades' equivalent of Dr. Spock, a Dr. Luther Holt of Columbia University, authored the best-selling parenting book of the time, *The Care and Feeding of Children* (East Norwalk, CT: Appleton-Century, fifteen editions between 1894 and 1915). In it, he warned parents of the adverse effects of the "vicious practice" of using a cradle, picking up the child when it cried, or handling the baby too often.

If parents were being told things like this, imagine how little incentive a nurse or attendant would feel to interact with a child, when confronted with a ward full of them in an orphanage or hospital. One pediatrician at Chicago's Children's Memorial Hospital instructed his staff to pick up and "amuse" each infant several times a day. Years later, he was still being cited as a maverick for having done so, for being an old softie so ahead of his time. And parents themselves were typically allowed only a few hours of visiting a week with an infant in a hospital.

By 1942, enough research on developmental psychology had been carried out for a correct explanation for hospitalism to be stated by a New York University physician named Harry Bakwin: "emotional deprivation." Or, to use a technical term that he introduced to the hospitalism literature in the title of one of his publications, "loneliness."

When an infant rat is licked and groomed by its mother, the pup secretes growth hormone, which triggers cell division—Mother's touch is essential for normal growth. In a series of remarkable studies, Michael Meaney and colleagues at McGill University have shown that being one of the lucky rats whose mother did a whole lot of licking and grooming resulted in an array of changes in the developing brain with lifelong effects—fewer stress hormones secreted as an adult, better learning under duress, probably delayed brain aging. Similar themes have emerged from primate studies, beginning with the classic work of Harry Harlow, who showed that infant monkeys understood development better than did the average pediatrician battling hospitalism—given a choice, the monkeys preferred maternal touch to maternal nutrition. And it was not sheer tactile stimulation that was essential. Harlow dared to inject into the modern scientific literature the word *love* when discussing normal primate development and what was essential. And in humans, a disorder of dramatically, even fatally disrupted development due to emotional deprivation can be found in every endocrine textbook on growth. It is called psychosocial dwarfism.

The infants in hospitals, despite adequate nutrition, a sufficient number of blankets, and various medical menaces kept at bay, wasted away from emotional deprivation. And as they became depressed and listless, their immune systems were likely to weaken (as has been shown for young nonhuman primates undergoing similar deprivation). Soon they'd be falling victim to the gastrointestinal or respiratory infections so common in hospitals at the time, at which point, the feverish medical enthusiasm for aseptic isolation would kick in. The pediatricians would see the infections as a cause, rather than an effect, of hospitalism, and the kids would quickly be consigned to isolated cubicles where the goal would be their never being touched by human hands. And the mortality rate would soar.

It all makes perfect sense now, and our contemporary explanation would be incomprehensible to the concerned and competent physician of that time, for whom battling disease began and ended with the germ theory. And why was there an inverse SES gradient to hospitalism? The punch line is scattered, here and there, in these musty papers. You can almost smell the confusion on the part of these experts, as they occasionally raised the issue of an odd pattern in the statistics—kids seemed to be less likely to succumb to hospitalism in the poorer hospitals, the ones that couldn't afford the state-of-the-art mechanical isolation boxes for marantic kids.

There are some lessons to be learned here. The specific lesson of hospitalism remains relevant. Modern medicine has developed an extraordinary ability to save premature infants, even those born months early and weighing a pound or two. But a prerequisite for such heroics is the neonatal intensive care unit, where, in the name of sterility, there remains a dearth of stimulation. In classic work done in the early 1980s, Tiffany Field of the University of Miami School of Medicine and colleagues went into such neonatology wards and started touching the kids: fifteen-minute periods, three times a day, stroking their bodies, moving their limbs. And it worked wonders. The kids grew nearly 50 percent faster, were more active and alert, matured faster behaviorally, and were released from the hospital nearly a week earlier than the premature infants who weren't touched. Months later, they were still doing better than preemies who hadn't been touched.

My sense is that this critical finding has yet to be implemented as widely as it could. And one does not have to look to the neonatal intensive care unit, or to ancient medical papers, to find something like hospitalism. Hold a needful, crying child in your arms, feel the comfort of comforting, feel the brief illusion that the world is a fair and safe place, and then think of warehouse stacks of children in those Romanian orphanages whose incarnations of hospitalism can take your breath away.

But there are some broader morals here. To quote Sholem Aleichem, while it's no shame to be poor, it's no great honor either. Try not to be poor. Maybe do something to help those who are. There's more to health care than vanquishing germs. There's more to normal development than adequate nutrition. And even if you're filthy rich, you still need to use sunscreen.

And there's a final moral, one that should sound merely cautionary, rather than like some antiscience rant. When we get sick, when a loved one does, when that inconceivable panic of mortality suddenly looms, the more proactive among us leap into action. We check the medical journals, check the health magazines, check *The National Enquirer,* take advantage of any connection, call that second cousin's ex-roommate who's the high-powered doc at the medical center—all to find out about the treatment that's the best, the *newest.* And the moral there is, every now and then, not so fast—the newest isn't always such a hot deal in medicine.

This isn't a very practical lesson, because medical mistakes aren't recognizable as such when they're first introduced. It's just useful to recall that, inevitably, once somewhere back when, a cutting-edge physician was able to inform a favorite patient about the newest—maybe it was applying a leech, maybe bleeding to release some vile humours, maybe a free sample of this new drug thalidomide. Or maybe it was the reassurance given to anxious parents that their sick child would be in a pediatric ward with all the most modern equipment.

⤳ NOTES AND FURTHER READING ⤳

The relationship between health and socioeconomic status is a huge subject and has been reviewed in these highly readable books by leaders of the field: Wilkinson R, *Mind the Gap: Hierarchies, Health and Human Evolution* (London: Weidenfeld and Nicolson, 2000); Marmot M, *The Status Syndrome* (New York: Scribner, 2004); Budrys G,

Unequal Health: How Inequality Contributes to Health or Illness (Lanham, MD: Rowman & Littlefield); and Kawachi I and Kennedy B, *The Health of Nations: Why Inequality Is Harmful to Your Health* (New York: The New Press, 2002). A review of the field can also be found in Sapolsky R, *Why Zebras Don't Get Ulcers: A Guide to Stress, Stress-Related Diseases, and Coping,* 3rd ed. (New York: Henry Holt, 2004), chap. 17.

The work on subjective SES can be found in Adler N, Epel E, Castellazzo G, and Ickovics J, "Relationship of subjective and objective social status with psychological and physiological functioning: preliminary data in healthy white women," *Health Psychology* 19 (2000): 586; Goodman E, Adler N, Daniels S, Morrison J, Slap G, and Dolan L, "Impact of objective and subjective social status on obesity in a biracial cohort of adolescents," *Obesity Research* 11 (2003): 1,018; and Singh-Manoux A, Adler N, Marmot MG, "Subjective social status: its determinants and its association with measures of ill-health in the Whitehall II study," *Social Science and Medicine* 56 (2003): 1,321. The literature on health and income inequality is reviewed in Wilkinson, cited above.

The nun study is reported in Snowdon D, Ostwald S, and Kane R, "Education, survival and independence in elderly Catholic sisters, 1936–1988." *American Journal of Epidemiology* 120 (1989): 999; and Snowdon D, Ostwald S, Kane R, and Keenan N, "Years of life with good and poor mental and physical function in the elderly," *Journal of Clinical Epidemiology* 42 (1989): 1,055.

Inverse SES diseases: Multiple sclerosis: Pincus T and Callahan L, "What explains the association between socioeconomic status and health: primarily access to medical care or mind-body variables?" *Advances* 11 (1995): 4. Melanoma: Kitagawa E and Hauser P, *Differential Mortality in the United States* (Cambridge: Harvard University Press, 1973). Polio: Pincus T in Davis B, ed., *Microbiology, Including Immunology and Molecular Genetics,* 3rd ed. (New York: Harper and Row, 1980).

Baboons and miscarriage: see Altmann J, Sapolsky R, and Licht P, "Scientific correspondence: baboon fertility and social status," *Nature* 377 (1995): 688.

The literature on hospitalism: Chapin H, "Are institutions for infants necessary?" *Journal of the American Medical Association,* January 2, 1915; and Chapin H, "A plea for accurate statistics in infants' institutions," *Transactions of the American Pediatric Society* 27 (1915): 180.

A review of hospitalism: Bakwin H, "Psychological aspects of pediatrics," *Journal of Pediatrics* 35 (1949): 512.

Holt's writings are discussed in Montagu A, *Touching: The Human Significance of the Skin* (New York: Harper and Row, 1978).

The maverick getting his staff to pick up kids: Brennemann J, "The infant ward," *American Journal of Diseases of Children* 43 (1932): 577. This work is also discussed fifteen years later in Bakwin, cited above.

Loneliness as a factor in hospitalism: Bakwin H, "Loneliness in infants," *American Journal of Diseases of Children* 63 (1942): 33.

Licking of rats: Kuhn C, Paul J, and Schanberg S, "Endocrine responses to mother-infant separation in developing rats," *Developmental Psychobiology* 23 (1990): 395. Meaney's work is reviewed in Meaney M, "Maternal care, gene expression, and the transmission of individual differences in stress reactivity across generations," *Annual Review of Neuroscience* 24 (2001): 1,161. Harlow's work is reported in Harlow H, "The nature of love," *American Psychologist* 13 (1959): 673, and is also reviewed in a superb biography of him: Deborah Blum, *Love at Goon Park: Harry Harlow and the Science of Affection* (New York: Perseus Books, 2002). Psychosocial dwarfism is reviewed in chapter 6, Sapolsky, *Why Zebras Don't Get Ulcers,* cited above.

Separation suppresses the immune system in nonhuman primates: Coe C, "Psychosocial factors and immunity in nonhuman primates: a review," *Psychosomatic Medicine* 55 (1993): 298.

Tiffany Field's work is reviewed in Field T, Schanberg S, Scarfidi F, and Bauer C, "Tactile kinesthetic stimulation effects on preterm neonates," *Pediatrics* 77 (1986): 654.

Finally, there is now developing a scientific literature documenting just how horrendous conditions have been for development in kids in Romanian orphanages. For an entrée to this field, see Gunnar M, Mirison S, Chisholm K, and Schuder M, "Salivary cortisol levels in children adopted from Romanian orphanages," *Development and Psychopathology* 13 (2001): 611. Warning: for anyone with children, this can be a heartbreakingly difficult literature to read.

The Cultural Desert

So a Swede and a Finn, two old friends, meet and decide to go to a bar. They settle down with their bottles of vodka and sit drinking in utter silence. Hours go by as the two drink away without a word. Finally, six hours into it, the Swede, somewhat inebriated and moved by life, love, and friendship, raises his glass to his friend and says, "To your health." To which the Finn replies, "Look, did you come here to drink or to talk?"

The joke was told to me by a Swedish scientist at a conference in Stockholm where we Yanks repeatedly teased the Swedes about their proverbial inexpressiveness: You think we're bad? You should see the neighbors. And yet *why* should Scandinavians be thought of as taciturn, and Mediterraneans as anything but? Why is it that Brazilians at World Cup matches are more likely to form a delirious explosion of singing, gyrating, painted faces, and outrageous costumes than the Swiss crowds? Why do schlocky wedding-band singers croon about girls from Ipanema but not from Düsseldorf?

All across the planet, where you live has something to do with the sort of culture you come up with. Traditional tundra societies are more likely to have cultural patterns in common with each other than with tropical-rain-forest societies (irrespective of whether those tundra societies descend from a common ancestral culture). High-altitude-plateau cultures are likely to differ in systematic ways from fishing cultures in island archipelagoes. Some of these correlations between

types of ecosystems and types of cultures are fairly predictable—
Tuareg desert nomads are not the sorts of folks who are going to have
twenty-seven different words for types of snow or fishhooks. But some
of the correlations are far from predictable and, as the main point of
this piece, have had a tremendous impact on the type of planet we
humans have produced.

Attempts to link culture with climate and ecology have an old history (Herodotus did it long before Montesquieu), but with the rise of
anthropology as a discipline, those attempts became "scientific" in
form if not in substance. Not surprisingly, the first attempts were often
anything but scientific, and were instead howlers of dead-white-
male racism that dominated anthropology early in the last century. In
other words, every study seemed to generate irrefutable scientific proof
that Northern European ecosystems produced superior cultures,
more advanced moral, technological, and intellectual development,
and better schnitzel.

Much of more-contemporary social anthropology represents a
traumatized retreat from the sins of those intellectual fathers, from
the invidious racism that formed the core of early anthropology. One
solution was to resolutely avoid comparing cultures with each other.
This ushered in an era where some anthropologist could spend an
entire career documenting the puberty rite of one clan of farmers in
northeastern Cameroon. Nevertheless, some anthropologists continued to remain generalists, studying cross-cultural patterns, tread-
ing cautiously in an effort to avoid ideological bias. And many
anthropologists continued to frame such cross-cultural work in the
context of how ecology affects culture.

One of the pioneers of the new and improved version of ecological anthropology was John Whiting of Harvard, who produced a
1964 paper entitled "Effects of Climate on Certain Cultural Practices." Comparing data from non-Westernized societies from around
the planet, he noted, for example, that husbands and wives from cultures in the colder parts of this planet are more likely to sleep

together at night than are spouses in the tropics. (However, Whiting gave no data regarding whether, in cold-climate cultures, it's the husbands or the wives who are more likely to wind up with the flannel blanket by the morning.) As another example, cultures in habitats that produce protein-poor diets have the longest restrictions on postpartum sex. Whiting figured that with protein-poor diets, infants were more dependent on extended nursing, which placed a premium on keeping births far apart.

Other anthropologists produced classic ecological studies concerning cross-cultural patterns of violence, in papers such as "Statistical Evidence for an Ecological Explanation of Warfare" (1982), by Melvin Ember of Yale. Ember determined, for instance, that certain ecosystems are sufficiently stable and benign that family units remain intact throughout the year, farming their plot of land or hunting and gathering in the surrounding rich forest. In other, more harsh and unstable settings, family units are often split up for long periods. During dry seasons, for example, preindustrial agriculturalists often have to divide their herds into smaller groups, with different family members scattered with subflocks to distant pockets of grazing land. In situations like those, you're more likely to have age-set warrior classes. There are advantages to a communal standing army, in the event that enemies show up when the men of your family are away finding grass for the cattle.

A radically different approach to cross-cultural research was pursued in the 1960s by Robert Textor of Stanford, who emerged as the factoid king of the field. Textor collected information on some four hundred different cultures from around the world and classified them according to nearly five hundred different traits. Was a particular culture matrilocal or patrilocal? What sort of legal system did it have? How did its people make a living? Did they believe in an afterlife? Did they weave, know about metallurgy? When at play, did they prefer games of chance or of strategy? Then he fed all these variables about all these cultures into some gigantic Stone Age computer and asked the beast to cross-correlate everything with everything else and spit out all the significant findings. The result is his monumental book, *Cross-Cultural Summary,* four inches thick, filled with table after table informing you, among other things, about what cultural differences are statistically likely to be linked to ecological differences. While not the sort of book you toss in your knapsack for beach reading, there is something irresistible about those thousands of pages of correlations. Where else could you discover that societies that don't work with leather will very reliably only have games of skill? How do you explain that one?

Amid all these different approaches, a basic dichotomy has emerged between two types of societies from very different ecosystems. The dichotomy strikes me as fascinating in its own right, but it also carries some disquieting implications for the sort of world we have created.

The dichotomy is between people who live in rain forests and those who live in deserts. Mbuti Pygmies versus Middle Eastern bedouins. Amazonian Indians versus nomads of the Sahara or the Gobi. The sorts of cultures they generate have some consistent and permeating differences. There are obviously exceptions, some pretty dramatic ones in some cases, but nonetheless, these correlates are reliable.

Some starters about religious belief. Who are the polytheistic animists, who are the monotheists? That one's easy. Rain-forest dwellers specialize in a proliferation of spirits and gods, whereas monotheism was an invention of the desert. This makes a kind of sense. Deserts teach big, singular things, like how tough of a world it is, a world reduced to simple, desiccated, furnace-blasted basics in every realm. "I am the Lord your God" and "There is but one God and his name is Allah" and "There will be no gods before me"—dictates like these proliferate. As implied in the final quote, monotheism does not always come with only one supernatural being—the world's dominant monotheistic religions are replete with angels and djinns and Satan. But hierarchy characterizes these religions, where the powers of the minor deities form only subsets of the uniquely Omnipotent One. In contrast, think of tropical-rain-forest people, in a world with a thousand different kinds of edible plants, hundreds of medicinal herbs, where you can find more different species of ants on a single tree than you would find in all the British Isles. Letting a thousand deities bloom in the same sort of equilibrium must seem the most natural thing in the world.

What's more, when you do encounter monotheistic rain-forest dwellers, they're much less likely to believe that their god sticks his or her nose into other people's business—controlling the weather, being responsible for illness, and so on. And this makes sense too. Rain forests define balance in both an ecological and cultural sense. If the forest pig evades your spear, there are endless plants to gather nearby instead. If an occasional disease wipes out one plant source, there are numerous alternatives. In contrast, in the desert, a locust swarm or an oasis that dries up can be a death sentence, and a world filled with such uncontrollable disasters inspires the famous fatalism of desert cultures, breeds a belief in an interventionist God with his own capricious plans.

The next big difference emerges from the work of Melvin Ember. Desert societies, with their far-flung members tending the goats and camels, are the classic spawning ground for warrior classes. And with them typically come all the accessories of a militaristic society: military trophies as stepping-stones to societal status, death in battle as a guarantee of a glorious afterlife, chains of command, centralized authority, stratification, slavery. A cosmology in which an omnipotent God dominates a host of minor deities finds a natural parallel in a rigid earthly hierarchy.

Textor's work indicates other correlates of desert versus rain-forest life. If you are a woman, you'd much rather stay away from those desert folks. The purchasing or indenture of wives is significantly less likely in rain-forest cultures. Moreover, such cultures are more likely than most to have matrilocal marital residence—related women form the core of a community for a lifetime, rather than being shipped off to wherever the expediency of marriage-making demands. Among desert cultures, women typically have the difficult tasks of building shelters and wandering in search of water and firewood, while the men contemplate the majesty of their herds and envision their next raid. In contrast, among rain-forest cultures, it's the men who are more likely to be doing the heavy work. And rain-forest cultures are less likely to have cultural beliefs about the inferiority of women; you are not likely to find men there praying thanks that they were not created a woman (as is the case in at least one notable desert-derived religion). Finally, desert cultures are likely to teach their children to be modest about nudity at an earlier age than in rain-forest cultures, and to have more severe strictures against premarital sex.

Which kind of culture would you prefer to get traded to? When it comes to the theistic part, it's six of one, half a dozen of the other for this atheist. What I don't believe in happens to be the Old-Man-with-the-big-white-beard-on-the-throne variety of god, but being atheistic about a bunch of forest spirits has a certain sixties, dancing-with-wolves appeal. As for the other cultural correlates, there's no question. Desert cultures, with their militarism, stratification, mistreatment of women, uptightness about child-rearing and sexuality, seem pretty unappealing. And yet ours is a planet dominated by the cultural descendants of the desert dwellers. At various points, the desert dwellers have poured out of the Middle East and have defined large parts of Eurasian cultures. Such cultures, in turn, have passed the last five hundred years subjugating the native populations of the Americas, Africa, and Australia. As a result, ours is a Judeo-Christian/Muslim world, not a Mbuti-Carib/Trobriand one.

So now we have Christians and Jews and Muslims in the wheat fields of Kansas, and in the cantons of the Alps, and in the rain forests of Malaysia. The desert mind-set, and the cultural baggage that it carries, has proven extraordinarily resilient as it has been exported by conquest and diffusion into these new and unlikely niches throughout the planet. Sure, there's not a whole lot of those folks still living like nomadic pastoralists, guiding their flocks of sheep with biblical staffs. But centuries, even millennia, after the emergence of these cultures, there is still the mark of those desert-correlated traits in the world they've fostered. Our scattered enemies, the Taliban, and our well-entrenched good friends, the Saudis, created societies of breathtaking repressiveness. In Jerusalem, in recent years, Jewish Orthodox zealots have battled police, trying to close down roads on Saturday, trying to impose their restrictive version of belief on the rest of their society. And for an American educator with, say, a quaint fondness for evolution, the power of the Christian right in many parts of this country to dictate what facts and truths may be uttered in a classroom is appalling. Only one way to think, to do, to be. Crusades and jihads, fatwas and inquisitions, hellfire and damnation.

Unfortunately, most evidence suggests that the rain-forest mind-set is more of a hothouse attribute, less hardy when uprooted. We have defoliated a world of forests, destroyed for slash-and-burn subsistence farming, commercial logging, clearing for cattle. This is an age that has not only seen an unprecedented extinction of species, but of cultures and languages as well, as the forest dweller's descendants are induced to acquire the lowest common denominators of this desert-derived world culture. As one measure of this, the demographer William Sutherland of the University of East Anglia has shown that the places on earth that have the most biodiversity have the most linguistic diversity as well, and those places where biodiversity is most threatened with extinction are where languages and cultures are going extinct at the highest rates. And thus the rain-forest cultures, with their fragile pluralism born of a lush world of plenty, deliquesce into the raw sewage of the slums of Rio and Lagos and Jakarta.

What are we to make of these correlations between environment and cultural beliefs and practices? Think of us humans as the primates that we are, and it makes perfect sense. Go and discover two new species of monkeys, never before seen. Know nothing about them other than that one lives in the trees of an Amazonian forest and that the other walks the arid scrubland of Namibia, and a card-carrying primatologist can predict with great accuracy the differing sex lives and reproductive biology of the two species, who is the more aggressive, the more territorial, and so on. In that respect, we're subject to the influences of ecology, just like any other species.

Two big things make us distinctive, though. First, our exceptions to rules are far more numerous and dramatic than you find in other primates. After all, that same mean ol' Judeo-Christian/ Muslim world that I've been ragging on has also produced Quakers and Sufis. In contrast, no olive baboon, amid the environmental constraints that favor omnivory in the savanna, has ever opted for vegetarianism as a moral statement.

The second thing that's distinctive about human culture is that we're not just talking about ecological influences on the kind of arrowhead you make, or whether, during some ritual in your culture, you shake some rattle before or after you do the dance with the hyena skull. What's at stake are some of the most central and defining of human issues. Is there a God or gods, and does your existence matter to them? What happens when you die, and how do your actions in life affect your afterlife? Is the body basically dirty and shameful? Is the world basically a benevolent place?

This far into the book, it should be obvious that if you want to understand how people find their answers to those intensely personal, individuating questions, you're going to have to let some biology in the back door. For example, we understand an extraordinary amount about the genetics, neurochemistry, and endocrinology of depression, about how those factors influence whether a person constitutionally views life as a vessel half-empty or half-full. And we are even beginning to glimpse a biology of religious belief itself—some types of neurological injuries cause religious obsessions, types of neuropsychiatric disorders associated with "metamagical" thinking; some brain regions regulate how tightly an organism demands a link between cause and effect in order for belief to emerge—potentially allowing for insight into that odd phenomenon that we call faith.

To answer the question, "How did I become who I am?" we must incorporate a myriad of subtle and interactive factors—from the selective pressures that shaped our primate gene pool eons ago to the burst of neurotransmitters a microsecond ago. Maybe it's time to add another biological variable to the list: When our forebears pondered life's big questions, did they do so while contemplating an enveloping shroud of trees, or an endless horizon?

⟶ NOTES AND FURTHER READING ⟵

The links between ecology and culture are covered in most standard anthropology texts. Some of the specific studies mentioned include Whiting J, "Effects of climate on certain cultural practices," in Goodenough W, ed., *Explorations in Cultural Anthropology* (New York: McGraw-Hill, 1964): 511; Ember M, "Statistical evidence for an ecological explanation of warfare," *American Anthropologist* 84 (1982): 645; Textor R, *A Cross-Cultural Summary* (New Haven, CT: HRAF Press, 1967); and Sutherland W, "Parallel extinction risk and global distribution of languages and species," *Nature* 423 (2003): 276. Also, for a great overview of this style of thinking for the nonspecialist, see Harris M, *Cannibals and Kings: The Origins of Cultures* (New York: Random House, 1977). Also, see Ember C and Ember M, in Martin D and Frayer D, eds., *Troubled Times, Violence and Warfare in the Past* (Amsterdam: OPA, 1997): 1.

A point of this piece was how, despite the considerable appeal of the typical rain-forest culture, as compared with the typical desert one, our planet is dominated by desert-derived Eurasian cultures. Why should this be? This has been considered by Jared Diamond in many of his writings, and in the greatest detail in his classic book, *Guns, Germs and Steel* (New York: Norton, 1997). His basic premise is that it's mostly been a matter of luck, of having the right types of animals and plants. For example, most of the world has some sort of wild sheep species, but only the Eurasian ones were easily domesticated, providing a fabulous food source. Most of the world has large wild bovids that would be ideal for labor, but the American bison and the African Cape buffalo have never been domesticated, whereas the Eurasian ones gave rise to oxen and cows. And the Eurasians had the luck to have horses to domesticate, allowing them tremendous military advantages—what a different world it would be if European empires had been toppled by a handful of conquistadores of color mounted on kangaroos or tapirs or zebras.

Finally, the penultimate paragraph makes reference to an emerging understanding of the neurobiology of religiosity. For an overview of some facets of that, see Sapolsky R, "Circling the Blanket for God," in *The Trouble with Testosterone and Other Essays on the Biology of the Human Predicament* (New York: Scribner, 1997).

Monkeyluv

Well, I have some terrible news for 99 percent of us never destined to make *People*'s Most Beautiful issue and thus get to be featured in essay one. This news is so terrible that it's even been reified with a cover story in *Newsweek*. But first, a Martian joke:

So the Martians finally come to Earth and they turn out to be great folks. Earthlings and Martians hit it off, sit around for days talking about politics, the weather on Mars and Earth, sports, what really happened with Elvis. . . . Eventually, both the earthlings and Martians feel comfortable enough to work up the nerve and ask the other folks what they're really curious about—"So how do you guys reproduce?"

It's decided to have a demonstration. The Martians go first. Four of them stand on top of each other, make whirring mechanical sounds, lights go off on their foreheads, smoke and bells, and . . . suddenly, a new Martian pops out.

"Fabulous, just fabulous, love the concept," say the earthlings. Then it's our turn. A suitable volunteer couple has been found, a bed cleared, and the couple goes at it while the Martians stand around taking souvenir photos. The pair finishes in a sweaty heap.

"Great, that was terrific, very novel," enthuse the Martians, "but one thing . . . er . . . where's the new earthling?"

"Oh, that," they are answered. "That happens nine months from now."

And the Martians ask, "So why were they in such a rush at the end?"

So why are we in such a rush at the end? We animals will swim upstream and leap over dams, will spend hours butting heads with other antlered beasts, will laugh at someone's stupid jokes, all for the chance to mate, to get into that special circumstance where we are in such a rush at the end.

What is it that drives us to do so? Is it for the good of the species? Nah—that style of thinking went out with Marlin Perkins. How about its being for the good of the individual? "By mating as frequently as possible, you maximize the number of copies of your genes in the next generation and thereby enhance your reproductive success in the general population pool." Yeah, right—how many animals bring evolutionary-biology textbooks to bed with them? Option three: Because it *feels* good. Of course.

What we have here is a dichotomy between the distal and proximal explanations for the same behavior. *Distal:* the long-term, underlying explanation for why something happened. *Proximal:* the short-term, nuts-and-bolts explanation. For example, a female primate gives birth to an infant and, against any sort of logic, exhausts herself caring for it, hauling it around, giving up calories and foraging time, making herself more vulnerable to predators with this cumbersome burden. Why toil away with this maternal behavior? Distal explanation: because among primates, high degrees of maternal investment increase the likelihood of survival of the offspring and thus maximization of passing on copies of genes. Proximal explanation: because something about those big eyes and ears with that wrinkly little face and, I can't stand it, that adorable round forehead, and you just *have* to take care of that kid.

Much of behavior is driven by proximal cues, and never is this more the case than when thinking about the motivation for sexual behavior. For behaviors that are that evolutionarily vital, that so often involve risk to life and limb, the motivation can't be abstract and delayed, like the consequences for genetic competition, or for the promise of offspring after a long gestation period (just imagine how few elephants there would be on earth if elephant sex were motivated purely by the cognitive recognition that, do this and, shazzam, two years later some kid pops out). Sexual behavior has to be driven, overwhelmingly, by proximal cues. Animals, including human beings, are interested in sex because it feels good.

Now that the Gentle Reader is clear about this fact, the question gets more interesting: What proximal cues are the most reinforcing for sex? Basically, what makes one organism sexy to another?

Remarkably enough, scientists have a pretty good sense by now of what qualities give us vertebrates the hots, and there are some consistencies across the animal kingdom. For starters, species from birds to humans seem to like the looks of someone who is average, symmetric in their face and build—the archetype of conventional beauty. People, for instance, can pick up incredibly subtle asymmetries in eyes, ears, wrists, or ankles, and those definitely count against a potential mate.

Why prefer symmetry? The generally accepted explanation is that this signals conventional health (although, as was the point of "Antlers of Clay," you should be cautious about automatically assuming that a case of healthy symmetry is due to genes). This attraction toward averageness accounts for a truly disturbing finding discovered soon after the invention of photography: if you superimpose the pictures of a whole bunch of human faces (or, nowadays, if you generate a computerized average of them), you get this really good-looking imaginary composite android face.

But certain outliers exert an even more magnetic attraction than the averagely healthy. In species after species, the proximal signals generated by females with higher than average appeal are ones indicating atypically high degrees of reproductive potential. Most males in most species respond to whatever their species' equivalent is of a woman with big-time child-bearing hips. And in the numerous species in which males are selected for traits that differentiate them from females, the exaggerated male traits that make hearts throb are those implying successful male-male competition—their equivalent of being buffed up, or possessing a territory or a high rank in a hierarchy. When taken to an extreme, the sexy male in many species is the metabolic equivalent of being economically well-endowed. As reviewed in "Antlers of Clay," this is the strange arena of secondary sexual characteristics among males, the enormous plumage, the wild coloration, the strange appendages. It is a sign of peacock strutting, of conspicuous consumption—"I am so healthy, so parasite-free, so well-off, that I can afford to waste all these calories on something as ridiculous as these huge neon antlers."

So throughout the animal kingdom, individuals of both sexes respond to the conventionally attractive all-American kid next door, but especially respond to the drop-dead gorgeous individual with the amazing _____ (fill in according to your species and gender). Those are the sorts of traits that provide particularly strong proximal cues toward mating. Now, the demoralizing fact confirmed by *Newsweek,* the one that all of us run-of-the-mill-looking folks knew all along, is that animals who generate those strong proximal cues get treated better. I don't just mean that good-looking vertebrates get to be more sexually active. They get treated better in all sorts of walks of life.

That's not news, of course, when it comes to humans. Study after study shows that we will listen with rapt attention to someone's raving gibberish, will preferentially give them a job or even vote for them, just because they have gorgeously symmetric wrists. The ones I'm really disappointed by are the nonhuman primates, who are usually more sensible than that.

A study by the ethologists Bernard Wallner and John Dittami of the University of Vienna shows a pretty egregious example of such preferential behavior among Barbary macaque monkeys. When a female comes into heat, she develops a conspicuous anogenital swelling that tells the world of her special ovarian status. Although the size of the swelling increases as a female approaches her ovulation day, some females have bigger swellings than others. And those females get treated better. When compared with females at the same point in their reproductive cycles who have smaller swellings, the well-endowed females are less likely to have males in bad moods displace aggression onto them. Moreover, males are more likely to groom them. Okay, so male macaques get gaga over pneumatic anogenital swellings. The ones who should *really* know better than that are the females. But they do it too—big-swelling individuals are preferentially groomed by females as well.

This is depressing as hell. Is there a phylogenetically widespread bias to treat individuals by how they look? Is all of evolution from slime molds on up one dazzling trajectory leading to the unlikelihood that Dan Quayle was once vice president? But it turns out that things may not be that bad after all.

A first example of some redeeming sensibility comes from an unlikely source, namely us humans. As discussed in "Antlers of Clay," the psychologist David Buss carried out a celebrated study concerning how people choose their mates, surveying more than ten thousand people from thirty-seven different cultures around the planet. As was noted, in every society studied, women placed a disproportionate emphasis in their mate preference for someone with good economic prospects. In contrast, in society after society, men disproportionately valued youth, someone who possesses the physical features that signal health and fertility.

Fair enough. But what was less reported was a commonality among the women and men of all these different cultures—highest on everyone's list was finding a mate who was kind and who loved them.

Isn't that sweet? Okay, let's be sour cynics for a moment. Buss was surveying what people look for in a mate, not whom they'd like to jump into the sack with right now. Ultimate issues, not proximal ones. Maybe when people are contemplating whom they want to grow old with, a sensible distalness predominates: it makes sense to go for someone who is kind, loving, capable of being a good parent, someone who will remember to put the cap back on the toothpaste. But when we put ourselves back into the realm of proximal cues, it might be that the person who makes your blood run scalding has none of those traits, has bad news written all over them. It seems unlikely that kindness is ever sexy.

Yet the evidence can be surprising.

In recent decades, a revolution has taken place in primatology. It had been thought that sexual behavior among Old World primates (the kinds that live in big social groups, like baboons or macaques) followed a "linear access" model: if a single female was in heat, the highest-ranking male would claim her. And if two females were in heat, males number one and two would mate with them, and so on. The mating patterns were assumed to arise exclusively from the outcome of male-male competition; the females passively wound up with whomever the competition allotted them.

The revolution was the discovery of "female choice," the wildly radical notion that females had some say in the matter. Maybe this had something to do with there having been a transition, such that the best primatologists around were female, and with their looking at the behavior of their animals without that linear-access bias. What was obvious was that some females didn't just passively wind up mating with whichever hunk strutted forward. Being half the size of males in many of these species, females couldn't convince a male they didn't favor to get lost by beating on him.

But they sure could fail to cooperate. Maybe a female wouldn't stand still when the male tried to mate. Maybe, when pursued by a male, she would repeatedly walk right past the male's worst rival, forcing the two into tense interactions. And with any luck, those two male rivals would get so haired out with each other that they would collapse into fighting, giving the female the opportunity to sneak off to the bushes and mate with the guy she is really interested in (a phenomenon called stolen copulations, as well as other, unprintable terms, by primatologists).

But if the female has a choice, who does she choose? Who does attract her to the bushes? The answer, at least among baboons, is stunning: the nice guy. Maybe it is a male with whom she has a "friendship," or a mutual grooming relationship. Maybe he carries her kid to safety when predators are around. Maybe he is the father of that kid. But basically, he is a male who is now favored because of the quality of the relationship he has worked out with her over time—not because he has won some fight with another male.

Let's be clear about what's happening. This is not the case of a female thinking, in effect, *Okay, that big hunk over there in the biker jacket is really hot, but be sensible, kiddo, the guy's trouble, better stick with kindly Alan Alda.* Just the opposite. These females are manipulating these big, dangerous studs into fighting with each other, are risking life and limb (as they are occasionally subject to fatal displacement aggression at the teeth of those frustrated males), all to sneak off to the bushes to have sex *with* the Alan Aldas of their society. Think about it: nice can be proximally sexy.

This is extraordinary. And even more extraordinary, genetic studies of paternity have shown that in some species, male primates who bypass overt male-male competition and instead covertly copulate in the bushes do pretty well for themselves in the task of passing on copies of their genes. By the coldly calculating bottom line of evolution, this niceness business is not just some foolish sentimentality; it's a successful strategy.

So let your average, callow primate get all crazed and libidinous over how someone looks or smells. For the monkey who actually cares about how he treats someone, the evolutionary payoff is at least as great. This is pleasing news on a proximal level: even for a nonhuman primate, the most erogenous organ can be the mind. Or the heart. And this is pleasing news on an ultimate level as well, for all of us who have been tempted to jettison our kindergarten lessons about being nice and sharing in favor of sad adult jadedness about looking out for number one. Maybe that notoriously asymmetric sage Leo Durocher was wrong with that business about nice guys finishing last.

The *Newsweek* cover piece, in all its depressing glory, was published June 3, 1996.

For a technical paper concerning the attractiveness of symmetry, see Kirkpatrick M and Rosenthal G, "Symmetry without fear," *Nature* 372 (1994): 134, while a good paper concerning the attractiveness of certain outlier features is found in Perrett D, May KJ, and Yoshikawa S, "Facial shape and judgments of female attractiveness," *Nature* 368 (1994): 239. For a technical article concerning the attractiveness of composite faces, see Etcoff N, "Beauty and the beholder," *Nature* 368 (1994): 186.

For the classic analysis of how fancy secondary sexual characteristics may advertise good health, see Hamilton W and Zuk M, "Heritable true fitness and bright birds: a role for parasites?" *Science* 218 (1982): 384.

For the report of female macaques getting treated better simply because of having big swellings, see Wallner B and Dittami J, "Postestrus anogenital swelling in female Barbary macaques. The larger, the better?" *Annals of the New York Academy of Sciences,* 807 (1997), 590.

David Buss's work: Buss D, *The Evolution of Desire: Strategies of Human Mating* (New York: Basic Books, 1994).

Female choice in the primate world is a key feature in Smuts B, *Sex and Friendship in Baboons,* 2nd ed. (Cambridge, MA: Harvard University Press, 1999). For an example of how the world of male-male competition is not a great predictor of reproductive success in an Old World primate, see Bercovitch F, "Dominance rank and reproductive maturation in male rhesus macaques *(Macaca mulatta),*" *Journal of Reproduction and Fertility* 99 (1993): 113.

Revenge Served Warm

Since well before the time of Dostoyevsky, people have thought about crime, and about punishment, and about their interconnections. Why punish society's miscreants? To keep them from doing future harm? To rehabilitate them? To deter future wrongdoers? To make the victims and punishers feel better? A paper published in *Nature* in 2002, destined to become a classic, shows an unappealing aspect of social behavior in action, and an unexpected good that can come of it.

Whether you are a diplomat or negotiator, an economist or war strategist, sometimes you have to decide whether to cooperate with someone, whether that person counts as a partner or an opponent. And as is familiar to animal behaviorists, the same question arises among social animal species that show cooperative behaviors. Just to pick a wild example, classic work by Gerald Wilkinson has shown that female vampire bats drink the blood of prey species (such as cattle) and fly back to large communal nests, where they disgorge the blood to feed the baby bats. They are then confronted with a strategic question: Do you feed only your own kids, your own plus those of close relatives, everyone's? Should your answer depend on what everyone else is doing?

These issues of altruism, reciprocity, and competition constitute the field called game theory. Participants play in pared-down mathematical games, with varying degrees of communication among the

179

players, and differing rewards for differing outcomes. Players must decide when to cooperate, and when, to use a highly technical term in the game-theory field, to "cheat." Game-theory analysis gets taught in all sorts of realms of professional training. And even more amazing, social animals have often evolved the most mathematically optimal strategies for when to cooperate and when to cheat—even without an MBA. Get this—even social bacteria have evolved optimal game-theory strategies for going about stabbing each other in their bacterial backs.

Suppose you have an ongoing game in which no one is cooperating, and no one can communicate. Suppose some players start cooperating. If enough of them do this, and especially if the cooperators can quickly find each other, cooperation would soon become the winning strategy. To use the jargon of evolutionary biologists who think about such things, it would "drive noncooperation into extinction."

So get cooperation going among a group of individuals and they're going to be in great shape. But despite this, whoever starts that trend, is the first to spontaneously introduce cooperation, is going to be mathematically disadvantaged forever after. This might be termed the "Whataschmuck" scenario. Amid the landscape of noncooperation, one addled soul does something spontaneously cooperative, and all the other social bacteria chortle, "Whataschmuck," and go back to competing, now one point ahead of that utopian dreamer. In this setting, random acts of altruism don't pay off.

Yet systems of reciprocal altruism do emerge in various social species, even among us humans. Thus, the central question in game theory is, "What circumstances bias toward cooperation, jump-start it into the range where it achieves a critical mass and vanquishes noncooperation?"

One well-studied factor that biases toward cooperation is if the players are related. This is the driving force behind a large percentage of the cooperative behaviors among animals. For example, among a variety of social insect species, there is such an outlandishly high degree of cooperation and altruism that most individuals will forgo the chance to reproduce, instead aiding other individuals (i.e., the queen) to do so. The late W. D. Hamilton, first introduced in "Antlers of Clay," revolutionized thinking in evolutionary biology by attributing such cooperation to the incredibly high degree of relatedness among members of a social insect colony. And a similar logic runs through the multitudinous, if less extreme, examples of cooperation among relatives in all sorts of social species.

Another way of jump-starting cooperation is to make the players *feel* related. This tends to be a human specialty, this process of "pseudokinship." All sorts of psychology studies show that if you stick a bunch of people together by arbitrary standards in competing groups (à la color war), and make sure they even understand that their grouping is arbitrary, they'll soon begin to perceive shared and commendable traits among themselves and a distinctive lack of them among the other side. At its extreme, this is what is exploited in militaries who keep groups of men in cohesive units from basic training to frontline battle, making these guys feel so much like a band of brothers that they're more likely to perform the ultimate cooperative act. And the flip side, "pseudospeciation," is exploited in those circumstances as well—make the other side seem so different, so unrelated, so inhumane, so unhuman, that it barely counts to kill them.

Another way of facilitating cooperation is if players play repeated rounds of the game. This makes sense. By introducing this shadow of a future, you introduce the potential for payback, for tit-for-tating the person the next time if that person cheated against you this time. And this reins in cheaters. That's why reciprocity rarely occurs in species without cohesive social groups—no krill gives away a hamburger today in exchange for being paid on Tuesday if the debtor is long gone by then. And it doesn't do you any good if the debtor krill is actually still around next Tuesday if you can't tell one krill from the other. Commensurate with that, vampire bats have among the largest brains of any bat species. Similarly, the primatologist Robin Dunbar has shown that among the social primates, the bigger the social group (i.e., the more individuals you have to keep track of), the larger the relative size of the brain.

Another factor that biases toward cooperation is if play is "open book"—when you face someone in a round of a game, you have access to the history of their gaming behavior. Here, you don't need the same individuals playing against each other repeatedly to select for cooperation. Instead, the introduction of reputation selects for it, in what is termed sequential altruism.

So relatives or pseudorelatives, repeated rounds with the same individual, open-book play, all facilitate the emergence of cooperation. And here is where a study, published in *Nature* in 2002 by Ernst Fehr and Simon Gachter, comes in. The authors set up a game with the worst conditions for cooperation to emerge. In a "one-shot, perfect-stranger" design, pairs of individuals played against each other. While there were many rounds to the game, no one ever played against the same individual twice. Moreover, all interactions were anonymous. No chance for payback to punish cheaters, and no chance of reputation emerging either.

Here's the game. Each player has a set amount of money, say $5. Each puts any or all of that $5 into a mutual pot, without knowing how much the other player is investing. Then a dollar is added to the pot, and the sum is split evenly between the two. So if both put in $5, they each wind up with $5.50 ($5 + $5 + $1 divided by 2). But suppose the first player puts in $5 and the second holds back, putting in $4? The first player get $5 at the end ($5 + $4 + $1 divided by 2), while the cheater gets $6 ($5 + $4 + $1 divided by 2, plus that $1 that was held back). Suppose the second player is a complete creep and puts in nothing. The first player has a loss, getting $3 ($5 + $0 + $1 divided by 2) while the second player gets $8 ($5 + $0 + $1 divided by 2, plus the $5 held back). Cheaters always prosper.

Now add the key element to the game. Immediately after this single, anonymous round, each player finds out the results, discovers whether the other player cheated. And then a wronged player can punish the cheater. You can fine the cheater, take away some of his or her money, so long as you are willing to give up the same amount yourself. You can punish cheaters if you are willing to pay for the opportunity.

The first interesting finding is that even with the one-shot, perfect-stranger design, cooperation emerges. Cheaters stop cheating. So cooperation becomes the dominant strategy in two different settings: first, when a bunch of players start spontaneously cooperating with each other, particularly with repeated rounds and reputation; second, when cheaters are punished, even in a one-shot, perfect-stranger design.

Now the really interesting part. The authors showed that everyone jumps at the chance to punish, to incur a cost to themselves to incur a cost to a cheater. And remember the one-shot, perfect-stranger design. Punishing brings no benefit to the punisher. The two players will never play together again, so there's no possibility that punishment teaches the cheater not to screw with you. And because of the anonymous design, the capacity to punish doesn't warn other players about the cheater. In the open-book setting, there is an incentive to pay for the chance to conspicuously punish, in the hopes that other players do the same, thereby putting the mark of Cain, if need be, on your next opponent. And various social animals will "pay" a great deal, in terms of energy expenditure and risk of injury, to punish open-book cheaters (and a way to *really* get that one going in an open-book world is to use an approach that evolved long ago in various military academies' honor codes, namely to punish those who fail to punish cheaters). But here, the act of punishing is as anonymous as was the act of cheating.

No logical good can come from the punishing in this game, but people avidly do it. Why? Simply out of the emotional desire for revenge. The authors show that the worse the cheater (in terms of how disproportionately they have held back in their contribution), the more others will pay to punish them—even among newly recruited players, unsavvy about any subtleties in this game.

Think about how weird this is. If a bunch of people were willing to incur costs to themselves by being spontaneously cooperative, that catapults you into an atmosphere of stable cooperation where everyone profits. Peace, harmony, Joan Baez singing as the credits roll. But people aren't willing to do it. In contrast, establish a setting where people can incur costs to themselves by punishing cheaters, where the punishing doesn't bring them any direct benefit or lead to any direct civic good . . . and they jump at the chance. And then, indirectly, an atmosphere of stable cooperation emerges from this frothy, emotional desire for revenge. And this is particularly interesting given how many of our societal unpleasantries—the jerk who cuts you off in traffic on the crowded freeway, the geek who concocts the next fifteen-minutes-of-fame computer virus—are one-shot, perfect-stranger interactions.

People will pay to get the chance to punish, but not to do good. If I were a Vulcan researching social behavior on Earth, this would seem like an irrational mess. But as a social primate, this makes perfect, ironic sense. Some social good occurs as the emergent, mathematical outcome of a not particularly attractive social trait. I guess you just have to take what you can get.

─◦ NOTES AND FURTHER READING ◦─

For a fascinating introduction to game theory and the evolution of behavior (particularly of cooperation), see Barash D, *The Survival Game: How Game Theory Explains the Biology of Cooperation and Competition* (New York: Times Books, 2003). The specific study discussed throughout this essay is Fehr E and Gachter S, "Altruistic punishment in humans," *Nature* 10 (2002): 415.

For an example of game-theory competition among bacteria, see Strassmann J, Zhu Y, and Quelier D, "Altruism and social cheating in the social amoeba *Dictyostelium discoideum,*" *Nature* 408 (2000): 965.

An example of Dunbar's work showing the relationship between the size of the cortex and the complexity of a social group in primates: Joffe T and Dunbar R, "Visual and socio-cognitive information processing in primate brain evolution," *Proceedings of the Royal Society of London,* Series B: *Biological Sciences* 264 (1997): 1,303.

Why We Want Their Bodies Back

L ast week I got a phone call that I've been waiting for since
1973.

That year I was sixteen, a student at an alternative high school in
New York City. All of us were wannabe hippies, jealous of our older
siblings who'd gotten to live the sixties. That summer there was a rock
festival upstate at Watkins Glen, what turned out to be the biggest
ever. Among the six hundred thousand who made the pilgrimage
were two of our friends: Bonnie Bickwit, with her peasant blouse and
bandanna, and Mitchell Weiser, with his ponytail. They met up at the
summer camp just outside the city where she was working, and
hitched off to the rock festival. And we never saw them again.

Everything we know about them said they hadn't run away. Something had happened to them. Throughout that fall, we talked to grizzled rural sheriffs and reporters. We spent our weekends posting
pictures of Bonnie and Mitch in the East Village in Manhattan, near
the buildings of cults that were rumored to kidnap kids. And then, the
nights after, we would have our nightmares about rape and torture
and murder. Their disappearance was one of the galvanizing events of
our adolescence, ultimately the longest unsolved teen disappearance in our nation's history.

And then last week the phone rang.

Mitch and Bonnie's classmates had gathered for a twenty-fifth
reunion. A ceremony had been organized to remember them, there'd

been some media coverage, and the right person watched it on TV. And called the police.

The story he told explained their disappearance, described their death by accidental drowning. The details were right, it made sense. And thus the phone rang with the news, e-mails rocketed back and forth among people who now barely remembered each other. And amid the muted excitement, we all kept coming back to the same issue: if this man's story was true, the bodies of Bonnie and Mitch should have been found. Show us the bodies, we thought, and the mystery will finally be solved.

The desire for tangible proof of the death of someone we know or love is a natural human impulse. But often that desire extends well beyond a purely rational need for certainty. In circumstances where there is not the remotest chance that someone is still alive, even where the dead died centuries ago, we still expend great energy, have lawsuits and diplomatic standoffs, even risk and lose lives, all to retrieve the dead. Consider, for example, the extreme risks taken by an international team of divers in 2001 to recover corpses from the sunken Russian submarine *Kursk*. Or as an immensely powerful example, for months after 9/11 our nation was brought to an awed silence by a version of this, the nearest thing we have had in generations to a holy national rite—the dangerous search for the dead at Ground Zero.

The quest to get the body back is a drama played out in an endless variety of settings. In Chile, for instance, where civilians of the wrong opinion vanished during the murderous reign of Augusto Pinochet decades ago, the now-elderly mothers of the disappeared still gather to demand—give us even a single bone of our children. Sometimes, the demand for remains crosses national or cultural boundaries and is passed down from generation to generation. A few years back, Spanish authorities (despite some local protest) returned the body of a chief to his native Botswana, more than a century after it was stolen from its fresh grave by colonial looters, preserved, and displayed in a Spanish museum. And the same desire is played out in the court battles between paleontologists and Native American groups: Does the scientific value of studying a skeleton outweigh the desire of a tribe to bury its ancestor? What is arguably the most extreme version of this ritualistic return took place a few years ago: in a 1597 invasion of Korea, the victorious Japanese cut off and preserved the noses of twenty thousand of their vanquished foe, and the whole lot of them were recently repatriated to Korea as a sign of reconciliation.

Twenty thousand noses? Lawsuits over a bone? The living dying to retrieve the dead? Why, in society after society, are we so obsessed with bringing back the dead? Why such ritualistic significance to a body?

Well, it seems obvious that our reverence for the dead should extend to reverence for their earthly remains, and the carrying out of rituals to put those remains to rest. "See that my grave's kept clean" goes an old spiritual. Even Neanderthal ritualistically buried their dead. Even elephants have their elephant graveyards.

Naturally, none of this turns out to be so simple. Some paleontologists now question whether the haunting image of the Neanderthal burial actually occurred. And while elephants do seem to have an eerie interest in their bones, will carry them for miles, cover them with vegetation, the graveyard is a myth. And human cultures differ dramatically as to their relationship to their dead. While most societies traditionally bury or cremate their deceased, others, such as the Masai of East Africa, discard them for scavengers. And even among cultures that bury their dead, our sense of a grave as hallowed ground is not necessarily shared. As late as the nineteenth century in northern Europe, burial was akin to leasing an apartment: graves were intermittently dug up and the remains discarded, to make room for the next tenants. And while the Western model of death involves grief and whispered respect, the Nyakyusa in Malawi have ornate funerary rituals of mocking the deceased.

Cultures even differ as to when they decide someone is good and dead. And sometimes, individuals whom we would consider robustly alive are considered dead. For example, in traditional Haitian society, if a person does something sufficiently taboo, the village collectively hires their shaman to turn the miscreant into a zombie—thereafter, the community believes he inhabits the world of the dead. Conversely, some societies continue hearty, active social interchanges with people we'd consider dead. In traditional Chinese society in Singapore, younger siblings have to wait their turn to get married, so sometimes an older sibling who dies unwed is betrothed in a "ghost marriage" to someone appropriate and deceased. And even in our own culture, with our obsession with bringing back the dead, with sufficient passage of time (and probably with the demise of the immediate kin of the deceased), the respectful act becomes just the opposite—while we consider it a moral imperative to try to retrieve the dead from the *Kursk,* doing the same to any skeletal remains on the *Titanic* would be seen as inappropriately disturbing the dead.

So much for the way we in our society do things as automatically constituting the human norm. Nonetheless, a huge number of cultures put their dead to rest in a somber and ritualistic manner and go to extraordinary lengths to retrieve bodies for such rituals. Why the obsession with getting back bodies?

The most obvious reason is to make sure the person really is dead. From Ulysses to Tom Hanks and his volleyball finally getting off that island, the "But I thought you were dead" is a time-honored plot device. Until the invention of the modern stethoscope about 185 years ago, determining if someone was dead or just in a coma was often difficult. That some people were buried alive gave rise to all sorts of adaptations to prevent this—Irish wakes (i.e., you sit around for days to see if the "corpse" wakes up), seventeenth-century laws that mandated a waiting period of days before burial, aristocrats who stipulated in their wills various ways that their corpses were to be mutilated (i.e., bodily insults meant to wake the not-dead). At its truly nutty extreme, this fear of being buried alive gave rise by the nineteenth century to patented coffins with escape hatches, and the German "dead house," where corpses, complete with little bells attached to the fingers, were stored until convincingly putrefied. Just in case.

So there's a long tradition of the dead occasionally turning out to be not so dead, and a decaying corpse is a pretty good way to rule out that possibility. I suspect that another reason for wanting the body back has much to do with the irrational energy that we put into denial. Beginning with our first toddler encounter with a dead robin in the backyard and our parents' uncomfortable "It's only sleeping," or with Grandpa going to the hospital and simply not coming back, our Western model of death is one of euphemism and denial, complete with our tiptoeing and whispering around the dead as if they really are just napping. As first demonstrated in the landmark work of Elisabeth Kübler-Ross, people in our society tend to react to tragedy—death, the news of terminal illness—with a fairly stereotyped sequence of stages, the first being denial (most typically followed by anger, bargaining, despair, and, if one is lucky, acceptance). To eventually reach that state of grace of acceptance, the denial must be passed—and thus the tendency of so many of us to consider it almost a bracing necessity, taking the bull of denial by the horns, to ask that the coffin be opened, to look upon the loved one's face. And you need the body for that.

Some of the time, we want the body back not so much to be convinced *that* they died, but more to learn *how* the person died. This can be a vast source of solace—"It was a painless death, he never knew what was happening." This can be the ghastly world of forensics, where sequence is everything—"She was already dead by the time X was done." Sometimes, the solace of "how" comes from learning something about the deceased by the nature of his or her death, the heroic act, the sacrifice that affirmed a group's values. In "A River Runs Through It," Norman MacLean wrote of the youthful murder of his hell-raising brother. He had been beaten to death by thugs unknown, and the autopsy revealed that the small bones in his hands were broken. And thus, "like many Scottish ministers before

191

him, [MacLean's father] had to derive what comfort he could from the faith that his son had died fighting." Similarly, many people were relieved to discover that passengers on the hijacked plane that crashed in Pennsylvania on 9/11 had apparently put up a valiant struggle.

The desire to get the body back is also sometimes associated with what we believe to be the spiritual well-being of the dead. The Tlingit of Alaska, for example, believe that a body must be recovered for reincarnation to occur. Among the Nuba of Sudan, men are circumcised only after death, and this is a prerequisite for an afterlife. A top-of-the-line Church of England funeral requires a body that can be blessed and put to eternal rest. Some cultures not only need the body, but *all* of the body. And thus Orthodox Jews saved teeth, amputated limbs, excised appendixes, for eventual burial, producing the recent image of Orthodox Jews in Israel combing the site of a terrorist bombing for scatterings of shredded flesh.

Another reason for wanting the body back is not for the well-being of the deceased, but for the well-being, spiritual or otherwise, of those in control of the body. In *Grave Matters,* a surprisingly entertaining book on cross-cultural aspects of death, the anthropologist Nigel Barley makes this point, writing, "The dead do not own their corpses." Funerary ritual, with the body as its centerpiece, is an unmatched opportunity to share, affirm, inculcate, and revitalize group values, while the funeral itself is a great setting to do politics, to shift alliances, to court, for mourners to gain honor with their piety and grief, for mourners to gain acclaim with the conspicuous consumption of the ceremony that they throw. A well-scripted funeral for a political martyr can galvanize potential crusaders into a self-sacrificing, homicidal frenzy. In a vast number of cultures, funerary ritual represents the triumph of the needs of the group over the needs, if any, of the deceased. And few settings match a state funeral as an opportunity for a government to signal don't-screw-with-us power and solidarity. Consider the seemingly odd act of the atheist Soviet Union of the 1920s preserving the body of Lenin in perpetuity like some Slavic saint. But, as Barley emphasizes, that was precisely the goal, the message to the great unwashed Russian peasantry—"We have crushed and replaced the Church"—thus spawning the weird ritual of deceased Communist pooh-bahs being mummified.

The group value of a funeral holds even when it is not for the mighty. Consider how we eulogize the dead. The overwhelming pressure is to say nice things, to glorify, exalt, and exaggerate the good acts of the person. This can sometimes involve some pretty selective filtering of memory, or downright invention if the person was a scoundrel or if the eulogist is a hired gun who didn't actually know the deceased. In our own society, the good acts that are acclaimed in funeral oration are drawn from a list heavily featuring fidelity, devotion to young children and aged parents, religiosity, a robust work ethic, and fondness for barbecuing. If on a certain level the concrete rituals of a funeral are lessons for the next generation—this is how you do it, remember that for when my time comes—the values eulogized represent a remarkably effective vehicle of conformity, producing that superego of a whisper in the ear of so many of us, "How do I want to be remembered?"

Thus, the pressure at a funeral to make the deceased seem like a saint. And when the funeral is for someone whom that society really does consider a saint, watch out. In this realm, Barley's dictim "The dead do not own their corpses" can stop being merely metaphorical. When Khomeini died in Iran, frenzied crowds of mourners were so eager to touch their beloved ayatollah that they tipped over his coffin and shredded his burial shroud. Barley tells the story of the death in 1231 of Elisabeth of Thuringia, someone so pious and clearly bound for sainthood that a crowd quickly dismembered her body for holy relics. Even more bizarre is the story of the eleventh-century Saint Romuald—in his old age, he made the mistake of noting plans to move from his Umbrian town; the locals, worried that some other burg would wind up with the holy relics of his body, promptly conspired to murder him.

The body can also be a vehicle for resolving cultural conflicts. After a small Japanese fishing vessel was accidentally sunk in 2001 by a U.S. navy submarine, the U.S. government mounted a multimillion-dollar effort to recover the dead. And as part of it, a professor of Japanese religion advised officials on the culturally sensitive wording to be used in military communiqués about the operation, and stipulated the ways and time of day that corpses would be raised and placed in body bags as to be in accordance with Japanese custom.

By contrast, sometimes a body can be a vehicle for one society to express values that are hostile to another society. There is a Maori tale of a man, grievously injured in battle, begging his comrades to quickly cut off his head and retreat with it, so that it wouldn't be appropriated, shrunken, and displayed as a trophy by the enemy. Recall the visceral power of the image of American dead being dragged through the streets by crowds of Somalis, or the American contractors recently ambushed in Iraq, their bodies burned and publicly hung. When Zaire's kleptocratic ruler Mobutu was in the final days of his dictatorship, he is believed to have spent his time exhuming the bones of his ancestors, so that they would not be desecrated by rebels. Likewise, even though there was no immediate threat of hostility when the United States gave up the Panama Canal, not only were the VCRs and microwaves packed up to be shipped back to the US of A, but so were the bodies disinterred from the American cemetery.

And this reason for wanting the body back should help to resolve an issue that keeps arising in these battles over Native American bones. Tribe X wants the museum to return the bones of their ancestors for burial. The scientists often retort, "But you folks don't even traditionally bury your dead." And that's not the point—the emotional force behind the Native American argument has to be "It doesn't matter what we do with our dead; if you white folks think it's critical to bury *your* dead, yet you think it's okay to put *our* dead in your display cases, then something's wrong here."

So amid the vast variety of human cultures, there are a large number of reasons to explain the desire to bring back the dead. To be sure that they are dead, to find out how they died. For the well-being of the dead, or the well-being, prestige, and propagandistic power of the living. To reaffirm a societal value or to keep a hostile society from affirming it. But it strikes me that there is an additional reason why we want the body back, why we want a full explanation of what happened. And this has to do with Bonnie and Mitch—our friends from high school—and the phone call that was finally made.

The caller, named Allyn Smith, was twenty-four at the time of the Watkins Glen rock festival. On the way home, he hitched a ride in a Volkswagen bus. A scrawny young couple were riding in the back, also hitching from the festival. Smith and the driver got stoned. It was a hot day, and a substantial river meandered near the highway. They stopped, planning to cool off in the water. As he was crouching down to take off his shoes, wondering at the wisdom of going in the water, Smith heard a shout. He turned to see that the girl had fallen in. The boy, her companion, leapt in to try to save her. And they were swept away, down the rapids, still very much alive.

This is the story Smith told the police. No names were exchanged in the van, but he had overheard the two talking about a summer camp where the girl worked, recalled identifying details about her clothes. No one else who had been to the festival was unaccounted for. It would appear that they were indeed Bonnie and Mitch. Smith is now cooperating with the police, trying to identify the road, the stretch of river. "I felt he was credible," says Roy Streever, the investigating detective with the New York State Police.

Many of us have some lingering skepticism—what happened to their backpacks that were in the van? Nevertheless, this probably is what happened. But just as important is what didn't happen next. Smith, tall, athletic, a navy vet, didn't try to rescue Bonnie and Mitch. He thought, "I ain't jumping into that, that's for sure," he told a reporter. Nor did the mysterious driver of the van. They sat there, wondering what to do. It is generally interpreted that they were hesitant to go to authorities because of their altered states. Eventually, they got back in the van, drove off. At a fork in the road with their paths diverging, Smith got out, and the driver said he'd report the two kids in the river to the police with an anonymous phone call from a gas station. Police have no record that a call was made, and no call was made by Smith . . . until the next millennium.

So, maybe it wasn't a murder after all, it was just a stupid accident—but where no one bothered to call for help for twenty-seven years. "When I asked him [why he waited so long], it didn't seem to bother him in the least," says Streever. "He just shrugged." One father and one stepfather went to their grave never knowing what had happened to Bonnie and Mitch.

And so a group of people has finally gotten the answer to a mystery from long ago. Once, we were kids who believed enough in our immortality that we'd hitch rides with strangers. Now, instead, we flaunt the same irrationality by cheating on our low-fat diets. Once, we had not yet learned that life brings tragedies beyond control. Now we wonder how we can spare our own children from that knowledge. And once, we lost two friends and could only imagine florid, violent sins of commission. And now, instead, we have had a doughy, middle-aged lesson about the toxic consequences of quiet sins of omission, of indifference.

Sometimes, when you get the body back, or at least finally find out the whole story, you learn something critical about the nature of the living, about those who knew all along what had happened.

⟶ NOTES AND FURTHER READING ⟵

The disappearance of Bonnie and Mitch was reported in a number of articles in *The New York Times* and the *New York Post*, 1973–74. The putative solution to their disappearance was reported in a series of articles (beginning 12/15/00) by Eric Greenberg in the *Jewish Weekly*;

they contained the quote by Smith. The quotes from Roy Steever were based on a number of phone conversations I had with him.

The revision about supposed Neanderthal burials can be found in Gargett R, "Grave shortcomings," *Current Anthropology* 30 (1989): 157, while the debunking of the proverbial elephants' graveyard can be found in Moss C, *Portraits in the Wild* (Chicago: University of Chicago Press, 1975).

Nigel Barley's book *Grave Matters* (New York: Henry Holt, 1995) contains information about the twenty thousand Korean noses and their repatriation, about funeral rituals of the Nyakyusa, Tlingit, Nuba, and Church of England, about the Maori warrior, as well as about "ghost marriages" among Chinese in Singapore.

Haitian zombification is the subject of Wade Davis's *The Serpent and the Rainbow* (New York: Warner Books, 1985). (This book, by a Harvard anthropologist, and reporting original research concerning the neurochemistry of zombification, was, nonetheless, sufficiently entertaining and tawdry to get turned into a really bad horror movie by the same name—the dream of every academician.)

The fear, in earlier times, of being buried alive and the various cultural adaptations that were meant to prevent it are detailed obsessively in Jan Bondeson's *Buried Alive* (New York: Norton, 2001).

Kübler-Ross's work is summarized in her classic 1969 book, *On Death and Dying* (New York: Macmillan).

The efforts of the U.S. Navy to respect Buddhist sensibilities were detailed on National Public Radio (11/8/01). Finally, the story about Zaire's Mobutu is told in Wrong M, *In the Footsteps of Mr. Kurtz* (New York: HarperCollins, 2000).

Open Season

Despite my best efforts to ignore him, my administrative assistant was getting on my nerves. Fresh out of college, Paul was working for a few years before starting English-lit grad school. It wasn't any problem with his work, which was superb. It was his taste in music. He'd be hunched over his computer, his CD recorder blasting away something horrendous by whatever group twenty-year-olds are listening to. That was fine; while it could be scientifically proven that his music was inferior to what my generation listened to, it was his prerogative to listen to nothing but that junk. What was irritating was that he didn't just listen to that. Sonic Youth for hours and then suddenly, late Beethoven. And then Grand Ole Opry. He kept switching what he listened to. Gregorian chants, Shostakovich, John Coltrane. Big-band hits, Yma Sumac. Puccini arias, Pygmy hunting songs. Philip Glass, klezmer classics. He was spending the first paychecks of his life in methodical exploration of new types of music, giving them a careful listening, forming opinions, hating some of the stuff, loving the process.

He was like that in all regards. He had a beard and longish hair, and then, one day without fanfare, everything was shaved to a bald pate—"I thought it would be interesting to try out this appearance for a while, see if it changes the way people interact with me." In his time off, he would spend a weekend at a film festival of Indian musicals, just for the experience. He'd pore over Melville, followed by Chaucer, followed by contemporary Hungarian realists. It was irritating how open-minded he was, how amenable to novelty.

It was more than irritating. It was depressing, because it made me reflect on my own narrowing. I listen to music constantly, but I can't remember the last time I listened to a new composer. It's even worse. I love all of Mahler, for example, yet I seem to only listen to the same two favorite symphonies all the time. The same for reggae, yet it's always the same trusted tape of Bob Marley's greatest hits. And if I'm going out to dinner, I've become more and more likely to be ordering the usual favorite.

How did this happen? When did it become so important to me to have solid, familiar ground underfoot? How did I become one of those people who buy "best of" anthologies advertised on late-night television?

For many people, this would be the point where one might do some soul-searching introspection, some painful confronting of truths as a means of personal growth. Being a scientist, I decided to avoid this by Studying the Subject. Donning my lab coat and positioning a microscope nearby, I started making phone calls.

I wanted to test whether there are some clear-cut maturational time-windows during which we form our cultural tastes, are open to new experience, even gravitate to it for its own sake. In particular, I wanted to determine whether there was a consistent age at which such windows of openness slammed shut.

As a CD of Wagner highlights played on ukulele boomed just outside my office, I wondered, When do we form our musical tastes, and when do we stop being open to most new music? My research assistants and I started calling radio stations that specialize in period music—contemporary rock, the "Stairway to Heaven" seventies stations, the fifties doo-wop stations, and so on. In each case, we would pose the same questions to the station manager. "When was most of the music that you play first introduced? And what is the average age of your listeners?"

After more than forty phone calls around the country, a pattern was clear: Not a whole lot of seventeen-year-olds are tuning in to the Andrew Sisters, not a lot of Rage Against the Machine is being played in retirement communities, and the biggest fans of sixty non-stop minutes of James Taylor are starting to wear relaxed jeans. This can be stated more precisely: when you put together the data sets generated by the two questions posed to the station managers, you get a fairly reliable measure of how old a listener of some sort of period music was when hearing that music for the first time. We found that most people are twenty years old or younger when first hearing the popular music they choose to listen to for the rest of their lives. When combining that with a measure of how variable those data were, we also observed that if you are more than thirty-five years old when some new popular music is introduced, there's a greater than 95 percent chance that you will never choose to listen to the stuff. The window has closed.

Giddy with those data, I turned to the sensory realm of food. At what ages are people most open to new foods? Psychologists have long studied gustatory novelty in laboratory animals, trying to understand how they choose their food, correct a dietary deficiency, or avoid a toxin. Many wildlife zoologists have had to start thinking about this issue as well when, thanks to habitat degradation, some wild population was forced into a new ecosystem. The anthropologist Shirley Strum studied a troop of wild baboons in Kenya, after farmers forced them off their native grounds, and watched the animals learn what plants in their new home were good to eat. The laboratory and field studies show the same thing: animals normally shy away from novel foods, and when they finally do get hungry enough to try out something new, youngsters are the most exploratory, both most likely to make a discovery and most open to changing their behavior when observing someone else who has.

Does the same thing work in us? Using the same time-window strategy as with the radio stations, I sought a food type that, by Middle American standards, was truly weird stuff, and that was first introduced during a recent identifiable time. Pizza? Bagels? No way, too pervasive. The transition from vegetable chop suey Cantonese food to spicy Szechuan food in Chinese restaurants? Not a clear transition point.

Sushi worked. Little pieces of raw fish with horseradish and bits of vegetable carved to look like flowers probably remain a bit off-putting to the pot-roast crowd living near those amber waves of grain. Returning to our phones, my research assistants and I started calling sushi restaurants throughout the Midwest, from Omaha, Nebraska, on up to Eden Prairie, Minnesota. When was sushi first introduced into your town? How old are your average non-Asian customers?

The news that a biologist from Stanford University wanted information for a survey generated some palpable consternation in some of these restaurants. We also stumbled onto what was apparently a nasty feud in Bloomington, Indiana, as to which of two sushi places opened first. But mostly, fifty restaurants later, we had a pretty clear pattern. Your average non-Asian, Midwestern sushi patron was twenty-eight years or younger when sushi first rode into town, and if you were more than thirty-nine at that time, the odds are greater than 95 percent that you'll never touch the stuff. Another window closed.

Emboldened further, I looked into one more category. I live near the Haight district in San Francisco, a neighborhood that makes this fortysomething realize just how many windows of novelty have shut closed in his mind. Thanks to this proximity, I was dimly aware that what is currently outrageous in fashion has changed a bit since we were affronting our elders by wearing jeans to high school. Here, surely, was another realm amenable to that time-window approach.

Tattoos wouldn't fit the bill for this study, in that they have been on the fashion scene consistently, and it is merely their connotations that have shifted. Pierced ears for guys have lost their power to make a statement—Dick Cheney could wear an earring and not have it bother his constituency, that's how mainstream it's gotten. Soon I had entered the world of tongue studs and navel and genital rings. Flee-ing to my office, I let my research assistant handle the phone calls alone on this one, calling body-piercing parlors. "When did you first start offering this type of body piercing in your town? How old is your average customer?"

Oddly, the news that the Stanford biology department was calling for this piece of information elicited not one raised eyebrow, pierced or otherwise. Apparently, people running these body-piercing estab-lishments require a lot to be surprised by something. Go figure. Thirty-five data points later, we had a remarkably clear answer. Your average denizen of tongue studs was eighteen or younger when that deconstructionist hermeneutic fashion statement, or whatever it is, made its entrance. And if you were more than twenty-three years old at the time, the odds are 95 percent that you'll pass up tongue studs, probably instead just trying to get a hairdo like Jennifer Aniston's.

Now we've got some major scientific discoveries on our hands. For at least one particular fashion novelty, the window of receptivity essentially closed by age twenty-three; for popular music, it closed by thirty-five; for an alien food type, by thirty-nine.

I soon discovered that, naturally, I had reinvented the wheel in my study—this pattern was already well recognized. One feature of this was the typical youthfulness of the creative process. Some professions are built upon the creative breakthroughs of virtually nothing but wunderkind—mathematics, for example. And other creative profes-sions show a less extreme version of the same pattern. Count the num-ber of melodies per year for a composer, poems for a poet, novel findings for a scientist, and on the average, there is a decline past a cer-tain, relatively youthful peak.

These studies also indicate that the great creative minds are not only less likely to generate something new with time, but are less open to someone else's novelty, the same phenomenon I was seeing in the sushi bar. Think of Einstein fighting a rearguard action against quantum mechanics. Or there was an immensely accomplished cell biologist named Alfred Mirsky who will go down in science history as the last major honcho in his field rejecting the idea that DNA was the molecule of heredity. As the physicist Max Planck once observed, established generations of scientists never accept new theories but, instead, die first. And in some cases, the closing of the mind involves an aging revolutionary repelled by what should have been the logical extension of his own revolution. Consider Martin Luther spending his final years helping to crush the peasant uprisings galvanized by the liberating effects of his mind. There's a consistent trend emerging here. As we age, most of us—the senior scientist flailing against his errant disciples, the commuter twiddling with the radio dial for a familiar tune—become less likely to be open to someone else's novelty.

What could this be about? As a neurobiologist, I turned first to trying to make sense of these findings in the context of brain science. The way that scientists used to think that brains age would easily explain the pattern I'd detected. In the old model, you'd be a teenager, and your brain was doing great, forming new connections among neurons, working better all the time. Then somewhere around, say, the very morning of your twentieth birthday, something would happen—that's it, you start losing neurons (ten thousand neurons per day, as everyone learned). An inevitable aspect of normal aging until, by age forty, your nervous system is neck and neck with that of a brine shrimp. And, in that view, this wasteland of dead neurons would have included parts of the brain involved in novelty seeking.

But this scenario has major problems. For one thing, the ten thousand dead neurons per day is an urban legend; brain aging doesn't involve massive neuron loss. The aged brain can even make new neurons and can form new connections between neurons. Nonetheless, the aging brain does appear to have a net loss of connectivity between neurons. That probably has something to do with why it's more difficult for us to absorb new information and apply it in a novel way as we age, while our ability to recall facts and apply them in the habitual way remains intact. But it doesn't explain the declining *appeal* of novelty: I don't think a whole lot of folks holding out for a good, thick steak do so because they have trouble understanding the raw-fish paradigm of sushi. And as a final problem with neurobiological speculations, there is no such thing as a novelty center in the brain, let alone subareas for fashion, music, and food that age at different speeds.

So neurobiology doesn't help much here. I turned to psychology. In a critical finding, the psychologist Dean Keith Simonton has shown that the creative output and openness to others' novelty among the great minds comes with a twist—the decline isn't predicted by the person's age as much as by how long the person has worked in one discipline. Scholars who switch disciplines seem to get their openness rejuvenated. It's not chronological age, but "disciplinary" age.

This might involve a few different things. Maybe the scholar changes fields, thinks in exactly the same stodgy way that has been producing clichés when he was still, say, a particle physicist, but it counts as fresh and new now that he has become a modern dancer. That wouldn't be very interesting. Perhaps changing disciplines truly does stimulate the mind to regain some of the youthful openness to novelty. The neuroscientist Marion Diamond has shown that one of the surest ways to trigger adult neurons to form new connections is to place the organism in a stimulating environment—this might have something to do with it.

An alternative explanation finds support in Simonton's recent work—for an aging person in a field, the thing that really does in openness to novelty, the real killer, is to suffer from the dread state of being . . . eminent. Novel discoveries in a field are, pretty much by definition, the ones that overturn the entrenched ideas of the intellectual elites. And thus, the reason that these gray eminences become reactionary is that a truly novel finding is likely to knock them and their buddies out of the textbooks—they have the most to lose in the face of novelty.

Meanwhile, the psychologist Judith Rich Harris has considered the problem in the context of humans overvaluing whatever group they are part of, and demonizing the out-group. In-groups are often defined by age, such as traditional cultures with age-set warrior classes, or Western education of kids by age class. So when you're fifteen, a key desire for you and your peers is to make it abundantly clear that you bear no resemblance to any age group that came before, as you seize upon whatever cultural outrage your generation has concocted. And a quarter century later, that same generational identification makes you cling to it—"Why should I listen to this new junk? Our music was good enough when we were defeating Hitler/liking Ike/having sex at Woodstock." People can be willing to die for the sake of group distinctions. Thus, they're certainly willing to listen to bad music for group distinctions.

Simonton's work begins to explain why, say, Johann Strauss would have fought the novel idea that it's pleasurable to waltz the night away to Arnold Schoenberg. And Harris's thinking may help explain why the generation that came of age waltzing to Strauss may not go for Schoenberg either. But as a biologist, I keep coming back to the fact that we humans are not alone in this pattern, and neither the eminence nor the peer-identification idea tells us much about why old animals are unwilling to try new foods.

Somewhere amid all this ruminating, it struck me that maybe I was asking the wrong question. Maybe the question shouldn't be why, as we age, we tend to disdain novelty. Perhaps, instead, it should be why, as we age, we crave familiarity. This is caught wonderfully in Tracy Kidder's book *Old Friends*. In it, a nursing-home resident comments on his forgetful roommate, "Heard only twice, Lou's memories could seem monotonous. Heard many times, they were like old friends. They were comforting." There's a stage of childhood in which kids become mad for repetition, taking pleasure in the realization that they are mastering rules. Maybe the pleasure at the other end of life is the realization that the rules are still there—as are we. As long as a likelihood of aging is that our cognition becomes more repetitive, it would be a humane quirk of evolution if we were reassured by that repetition. As Igor Stravinsky lay dying, he repeatedly banged his ring against the metal railing of his hospital bed, startling his wife each time. Finally, a little irritated, she asked why he was doing that, since he knew she was still there. "But I want to be sure that *I* still exist," he replied. Perhaps the repetition and comfort of traversing known, solid ground is our banging on the railing.

What all scientists are supposed to say right now is "Clearly, more research is needed on this subject." But does our closing to novelty really matter? It would be a good thing to figure how to keep our most creative thinkers creating longer. But is a major societal problem our paucity of eighty-year-olds with tongue studs eating raw eel? Is it a crime if I keep listening to that Bob Marley tape? There may even be some advantages for social groups to have the aging become protective archivists of what was, instead of constantly jettisoning the old to soak up the new. The physiologist Jared Diamond has argued that part of the success of Cro-Magnons was that they lived about 50 percent longer than did Neanderthals—when some rare ecologic catastrophe hit, they had a 50 percent greater chance of someone being old enough to remember the last time that happened and how they got out of that mess. Perhaps in my old age when there's a locust infestation that devastates food stores at my university, I'll be able to save the young'uns with memories of which wild plants behind the Student Union are safe to eat (with an ancillary lecture on the side about how reggae isn't what it used to be).

But if I stopped being Joe Scientist for a moment and actually reflected on some of this stuff, I find it a little dispiriting. An impoverishment comes with the narrowing, with this closing to novelty and glorying at repetition. What a shock, the discovery that by age forty you've already been dipped in bronze and placed on a mantelpiece, that there are already societal institutions like oldies radio stations whose very existence affirms that you are no longer where culture is. If there's a rich, vibrant, new world out there, it shouldn't be just for twenty-year-olds to explore for exploration's sake. Whatever it is that fends us off from novelty, I figure maybe it's worth putting up a bit of a fight, even if it means forgoing Bob Marley every now and then. But there's another, ultimately even more important consequence of this narrowing. When I see the finest of my students agitated over a cause, when I see them ready to go to the other end of the Earth to minister to lepers in the Congo, or to go to the other side of town to teach some kid in the barrio how to read, I remember—once, it was so much easier to be that way. An open mind is a prerequisite to an open heart.

—⟡ NOTES AND FURTHER READING ⟡—

More thorough documentation of how people, both highly creative and run-of-the-mill, and from all sorts of cultures around the world, close to novelty as they age can be found in the work of the gerontologist Robert McCrae (who shows, among other things, how much this occurs long before we become geriatric): McCrae R, "Openness to experience as a basic dimension of personality," *Imagination, Cognition and Personality* 13 (1993): 39.

The typical closing to novelty of highly creative individuals as they age has been documented in Simonton D, *Genius, Creativity, and Leadership: Historiometric Inquiries* (Cambridge, MA: Harvard University Press, 1984). A good, nontechnical summary of Marian Diamond's encouraging work can be found in Diamond MC, "Enrichment, response of the brain," *Encyclopedia of Neuroscience,* 3rd ed. (Amsterdam: Elsevier Science, 2001). The revolution concerning new neurons in the adult brain is reviewed in Gould E and Gross C, "Neurogenesis in adult mammals: some progress and problems," *Journal of Neuroscience* 22 (2002): 619.

Simonton's findings regarding eminence can be found in his book cited above. Harris's work is best summarized in Harris JR, *The Nurture Assumption* (New York: The Free Press, 1998).

The Kidder quote is from Kidder T, *Old Friends* (New York: Houghton Mifflin, 1993). The Stravinsky quote can be found in Craft R, *Stravinsky: The Chronicle of a Friendship, 1948–1971* (New York: Knopf, 1972). Jared Diamond's ideas can be found in Diamond J, *The Third Chimpanzee* (New York: HarperCollins, 1992).

Throughout the piece, I kept discussing how, *on the average,* people *tend* to close to novelty as they age—there are, of course, dramatic exceptions. Some fascinating work has been done by the historian of science Frank Sulloway, looking at who the exceptions are. Some factors that seem to increase the likelihood of remaining open to an intellectual revolution include not being firstborn, having a contentious relationship with your parents (particularly fathers, amid the overwhelmingly male population of scientists that he studied), being raised in a socially progressive home, and extensive experiences of foreign cultures in your youth. These ideas are summarized in his immensely provocative book *Born to Rebel* (New York: Random House, 1998).

The nicest thing about publishing this piece was getting to find out firsthand about the dramatic exceptions out there to this aging pattern—afterward, I heard from all sorts of octogenarians, taking a minute before their hang-gliding lesson to e-mail me about how they sure didn't fit the pattern I'd written about. That's great.

And as for my own closing to cultural novelty? Prompted by carrying out this study and with advice from Paul, my assistant, I started listening to the music of someone who was certifiably of his generation, and not mine. It was terrific; I love it, listen to it all the time now. But I noted that by that mere act, I destroyed the cachet of trendiness that the music had among the students in my lab—none of them would be caught dead listening to it now. So this artist will go unnamed, in the interest of not ruining the person's career.